my **revisi⊙n** notes

AQA GCSE (9–1)

CITIZENSHIP STUDIES

SECOND EDITION

Mike Mitchell

HODDER
EDUCATION
AN HACHETTE UK COMPANY

The Publishers would like to thank the following for permission to reproduce copyright material.

Photo credits

p.71 © False Economy

Acknowledgements

p.22 Reprinted with permission of NSPCC (https://www.nspcc.org.uk/what-we-do/campaigns/order-in-court/); **p.45** Turnout by age in the 2017 General Election and How people voted by age in the 2017 General Election. Reprinted with permission of YouGov.

Every effort has been made to trace all copyright holders, but if any have been inadvertently overlooked, the Publishers will be pleased to make the necessary arrangements at the first opportunity.

Although every effort has been made to ensure that website addresses are correct at time of going to press, Hodder Education cannot be held responsible for the content of any website mentioned in this book. It is sometimes possible to find a relocated web page by typing in the address of the home page for a website in the URL window of your browser.

Hachette UK's policy is to use papers that are natural, renewable and recyclable products and made from wood grown in sustainable forests. The logging and manufacturing processes are expected to conform to the environmental regulations of the country of origin.

Orders: please contact Bookpoint Ltd, 130 Park Drive, Milton Park, Abingdon, Oxon OX14 4SE. Telephone: (44) 01235 827720. Fax: (44) 01235 400401. Email education@bookpoint.co.uk. Lines are open from 9 a.m. to 5 p.m., Monday to Saturday, with a 24-hour message answering service. You can also order through our website: www.hoddereducation.co.uk

ISBN: 978 1 5104 1830 1

© Mike Mitchell 2018

First published in 2012
This second edition published in 2018 by
Hodder Education,
An Hachette UK Company
Carmelite House
50 Victoria Embankment
London EC4Y 0DZ

www.hoddereducation.co.uk

Impression number   10 9 8 7 6 5 4 3

Year   2022 2021 2020 2019 2018

Cover photo © Kirstypargeter/Thinkstock/iStock/Getty Images

Illustrations by Integra

Typeset in Bembo Std Regular 11/13 by Integra Software Services Pvt. Ltd., Pondicherry, India

Printed in India

A catalogue record for this title is available from the British Library.

Get the most from this book

Everyone has to decide his or her own revision strategy, but it is essential to review your work, learn it and test your understanding. These Revision Notes will help you to do that in a planned way, topic by topic. Use this book as the cornerstone of your revision and don't hesitate to write in it – personalise your notes and check your progress by ticking off each section as you revise.

Tick to track your progress

Use the revision planner on pages 4–6 to plan your revision, topic by topic. Tick each box when you have:

- revised and understood a topic
- tested yourself
- practised the exam questions and gone online to check your answers.

You can also keep track of your revision by ticking off each topic heading in the book. You may find it helpful to add your own notes as you work through each topic.

Features to help you succeed

Exam tips

Expert tips are given throughout the book to help you polish your exam technique in order to maximise your chances in the exam.

Now test yourself

These short, knowledge-based questions provide the first step in testing your learning. Answers are online at **www.hoddereducation.co.uk/myrevisionnotes**

Definitions and key words

Clear, concise definitions of essential key terms are provided where they first appear. Key words are highlighted in bold throughout the book.

Exam practice

Practice exam questions are provided for each topic. These are written in the same style as the examination questions that you will face in the real examinations. Use them to consolidate your revision and practise your exam skills.

Websites

Carry out some further research and make sure you have the up-to-date information and knowledge to take into the exam.

Online

Go online to check your answers to the 'Now test yourself' and exam questions at **www.hoddereducation.co.uk/myrevisionnotes**

My revision planner

My Revision Notes: AQA GCSE (9–1) Citizenship Studies is written to help you progress your revision and is written in the same sequence as the examination papers you will complete.

Paper 1 Section A: Active citizenship

REVISED   TESTED   EXAM READY

REVISED TESTED EXAM READY

REVISED   TESTED   EXAM READY

Paper 2 Section B: Rights and responsibilities

REVISED TESTED EXAM READY

More help and advice available online at www.hoddereducation.co.uk/myrevisionnotesdownloads.

As well as specimen answers to all the questions in this book there are also two chapters which will help you understand more about the specification and the assessment structure of the two GCSE examination papers. The second chapter is about the citizenship skills and processes that underpin this specification.

For example, in three of the four sections of the examination paper you are asked a synoptic question. These 8 mark questions have an* next to them. By referring to the online chapter about assessment you will find guidance about synoptic questions and how to answer them.

Answers to 'Now test yourself' and exam practice questions at
www.hoddereducation.co.uk/myrevisionnotesdownloads

1 Making a difference in society

Chapters 1, 2 and 3 are about how citizens can take part in society and try to make a difference. These three chapters look at the content covered in the concluding section of each of the three themes in the specification:

- Life in modern Britain
- Politics and participation
- Rights and responsibilities.

You are assessed on this content in Section A of Paper 1.

Opportunities and barriers to citizen participation in democracy

REVISED

Opportunities

Within a **democracy** like the UK, citizens have the right to participate in a variety of ways in issues that concern them. Some are formalised as a part of the political/democratic process:

- Voting for or access to elected members like **councillors, Police and Crime Commissioners** and **Members of Parliament (MPs)**
- Standing for election
- Using e-democracy formats to set up online petitions on issues that may be discussed by the UK Parliament.

Citizens can also access the legal system and try to get the judiciary to make a decision about an issue that concerns them. They can work with others in pressure or interest groups to bring about change.

Increasingly citizens, especially younger people, are participating in a more informal approach to bring about change. Rather than formally joining groups, they participate by supporting campaigns especially via the internet and the use of social media. The internet, through websites like 38 Degrees, is bringing people, causes and campaigns together to exert pressure to bring about change. 38 Degrees was instrumental in getting the UK Parliament to vote down proposed **legislation** to privatise the state-owned forests in the UK.

Barriers

People who do not participate give a wide range of reasons why they do not do so:

- Lack of interest or apathy
- Belief that their participation will not make a difference
- Lack of faith in politicians and the political process
- Lack of information or knowledge of the skills about how to participate
- The issues are not important to them
- They lead busy lives so don't have the time to participate.

Some attempts have been made to make voting and registering to vote easier, but many of the points above relate to the motivation or interest of the individual. This was one of the reasons why Citizenship was introduced as a compulsory National Curriculum subject: to introduce

Democracy – a political system based upon the concept of people having the power to decide. The word comes from the ancient Greek for 'people' and 'power'.

Councillors – citizens who are elected to serve on local councils.

Police and Crime Commissioners – directly elected officials who are responsible for the running of each regional police force outside London.

Member of Parliament (MP) – a citizen elected to Parliament who serves as a Member of Parliament, normally as a member of a political party.

Legislation – or statute law; laws passed by Parliament.

students to the nature of participation in a democratic society. Also the introduction of **National Citizenship Service** has led to more young people being involved in the voluntary sector.

Suggestions to increase **voter turnout** include:
- compulsory voting
- lowering the voting age to 16
- allowing online voting.

It does appear that, if people and especially young people are motivated about an issue, they will take part. The referendum on Scottish independence in 2014 shows that, when people think their vote will make a difference and the issue they are voting about is clearly defined, they are prepared to take part. In this referendum, 16- and 17-year-olds were able to vote and over 109,000 in that age group registered to vote. Overall, the referendum turnout was 84.6 per cent (see Table 1.1).

National Citizenship Service – a locally based government initiative that encourages young people to volunteer.

Voter turnout – the number of voters who actually vote, against the total number who could vote, normally expressed as a percentage.

Table 1.1 Percentage of 18–24-year-olds who voted in General Elections, 2010–2017

UK General Election	% of 18–24-year-olds who voted
2010	52
2015	38
2017	57

Many of the old perceptions about young people and participation are now being questioned. Table 1.1 shows that young people did become engaged during the 2017 General Election and did vote. Gradually the barriers to participation appear to be coming down; this may be due to the increasing influence of the internet, the ability to source news and opinion relevant to the individual and the ability to make your voice heard through social media and internet campaigning 24/7.

Actions to hold those in power to account

REVISED

Table 1.2 Advantages and disadvantages of the main forms of citizen action

Form of citizen action	Advantages	Disadvantages
Joining an interest group	Provides a focus for a limited range of objectives	Normally interest groups are not campaigning groups; also their field of interest can be very narrow
Joining a political party	Enables a person to fully participate in the political process	By joining they are governed by the rules of the party, so do not have total freedom of action
Standing for election	If the candidate standing is wearing a political label they have to support the views of the party An independent candidate is less likely to get elected but is able to speak and vote on issues as they wish	They can become a part of the system and find that the power to influence decision locally is limited
Campaigning	Campaigners become fully involved with the issue and motivated to bring about a change Helps improve a range of skills	Campaigners can move from acceptable to unacceptable forms of action An issue/campaign can become a dominant factor in their life

➔

Form of citizen action	Advantages	Disadvantages
Advocacy	Excellent skill to develop, enabling the participant to present a point of view clearly to an audience both in favour of and against their point of view	The skill could overcome the cause, so that the advocacy lacks sincerity
Lobbying	Excellent campaigning skill to acquire Provides the ability to know who to contact about an issue and how to present a case	Those who are lobbied often see this as a part of the campaigning process and believe that the views only represent a sectional viewpoint
Petitions	Collecting vast numbers of signatures does indicate the level of public support for a campaign It is easy to organise and a low-cost campaigning tool	These are increasingly completed online and it is easy to collect support, so they can often be disregarded The government's e-petition system undermines other types of petitioning
Joining a demonstration	A way of feeling committed to a campaign and being actively involved It only requires being in the right place at the right time	If the demonstration gets out of hand disruption and violence can occur and demonstrators can place themselves in danger of injury or arrest
Volunteering	Gives one a sense of helping others or a cause	It does not in itself promote a change in a campaigning sense

The role of organisations

REVISED

Table 1.3 shows how organisations such as public services, interest groups, **pressure groups**, **trade unions**, charities and voluntary groups play a role in providing a voice and support for different groups in society.

> **Pressure groups** – organised bodies of citizens who share a common interest in an issue and through a variety of actions promote their cause.
>
> **Trade unions** – employment-based groups of employees who seek to represent workers in regard to their conditions of employment, such as wages. An example would be the RMT (the National Union of Rail, Maritime and Transport Workers), which represents amongst others those working on the London Underground.
>
> **Trades Union Congress (TUC)** – a national body that represents most trade unions in the UK.

Table 1.3 Examples of organisations that provide support for different groups in society

Body	Role in providing a voice for different groups
Public services Definition: State service providers at a national or local level, e.g the NHS, schools, social services, libraries.	While public sector service providers have direct contact with the public and provide a service, increasingly there are linked support services that enable the public to raise concerns or issues they have regarding public service provision. There are ombudsmen for the health service, local government and the work of central government through the parliamentary ombudsman. Local and national government fund a large number of bodies with grants such as housing associations, Citizens Advice and other voluntary groups that provide a voice and services for those in need.

Body	Role in providing a voice for different groups
Pressure groups Definition: Groups of people who work and campaign together regarding specific issues to bring about change or maintain the current situation.	Pressure groups can be local, national or global. Not all pressure groups operate in the same way. They are classified in different ways by their status, the nature of the issue they are concerned about or the methods they use. **Single-cause groups**: These pressure groups focus on a single issue: for example, those opposed to the HS2 high-speed rail development. **Multi-cause groups**: These are groups that seek to influence policy and decisions over a range of issues, such as trade unions that seek to influence policy on pay, hours of work, health and safety, pensions, discrimination, etc: for example, the RMT trade union. **Protective**: These are groups that seek to protect the interests of their members: for example, the British Medical Association, which is the professional body that speaks on behalf of doctors. **Promotional**: These are groups that wish to promote views to their members and other interested parties on a particular topic: for example, Greenpeace is interested in environmental issues. Groups are also classified by their status as insider or outsider groups: ● Insider status implies that the group is able to discuss with, meet and be consulted by those it wishes to influence. For example, if there were to be changes to rural planning regulations the government would consult the Campaign to Protect Rural England (CPRE) but would be unlikely to involve the Countryside Alliance, which is seen as an outsider group, in direct talks or negotiations. ● Outsider status implies that the group does not have direct access to those making decisions and is not consulted or directly involved in discussions. These groups often seek outsider status, not wishing to be a part of the 'system' of talks and negotiations. ● They are deemed to be outsiders because the methods they use often involve direct action. Fathers4Justice was labelled an outsider group.
Trade unions Definition: These are organisations of workers within the same occupational field who pay to belong to the trade union that seeks to represent them in regard to pay and conditions of service with their employers.	Trade unions seek to provide a voice for their members, protecting their right within the workplace and negotiating with employers. As a collective body they can speak on behalf of millions. Many trade unions also work through the **Trades Union Congress (TUC)** to lobby government on behalf of all their members on work-related issues or matters of public policy, such as pensions, welfare benefits or labour market proposed legislation.
Charities Definition: The term refers to a legal status granted by the state that allows a body or organisation certain legal rights and also gives some taxation benefits. The Charity Commission approves applications that meet the criteria and monitors the work of charities.	Charities help specific groups in society, be they children, adults, animals or a building or institution. They can be local or concerned with national issues. The NSPCC and RSPCA are two well-known national charities. Many originated many years ago to look after groups that society didn't protect.

➜

Body	Role in providing a voice for different groups
Voluntary groups Definition: These groups may or may not be registered charities. They are groups of people working together locally or nationally to assist those in need. Unlike pressure groups whose purpose is to campaign, a voluntary group normally provides a service/assistance but will seek to campaign/promote its own work.	Voluntary groups can be very small and relate to a village or a community, or a national group. By their nature they seek assistance from citizens to help them provide a service to others. One might volunteer to help at a luncheon club or hear children read in the library.

How citizens work together to change communities

REVISED

In the examination you may be asked to discuss a case study of citizens working together in their community. You should have studied two during the course. As this is community based ideally you should relate this to your own local community, as you are best placed to write about the context of where you live, but other examples of community activity are acceptable. The case study below is of a tragic story that dominated the news in summer 2017, and provides a template for how you might research and revise for this topic.

Case study: The Grenfell Tower fire

The fire was reported at 00.54 on Wednesday 14 June 2017; 40 fire engines and 200 firefighters attended the blaze. It took nearly 24 hours to get the blaze under control in the 24-storey block of flats. At least 86 people are believed to have died and hundreds were made homeless. The police are investigating to see if any charges need to be brought regarding the safety of the building.

The local community rallied round and many volunteered to offer help, food, accommodation and support. The local council was criticised for the way it approached the crisis. The community has formed action groups to ensure that those responsible are held to account. Tests have been carried out on high-rise and other public buildings in the UK to see if they have sufficient fire protection. The government has launched a formal public inquiry into the fire. Politicians have said that public policy regarding attitudes to social housing needs to be addressed.

Arising from this one very tragic event, we see the formation of strong community groups, questioning of the role of local government, pressure on central government and a national feeling that this must never happen again and that everybody needs to be able to feel safe and secure within their own home.

Grenfell Tower Action Group

An action group that warned of fire risks at Grenfell Tower seven months before the fire has branded the council and the building's management 'complacent, negligent and incompetent'. In a scathing blog post, Grenfell Tower Action Group raised a number of fire safety issues in the building over the years. In the post, they said: 'The many who lost their lives in this catastrophe were our friends and neighbours. We tried to speak for them in life and we will continue to speak for them now.'

The next case study shows how a group of students concerned about the welfare of fellow students campaigned on their behalf; they managed to attract local media coverage and the support of local MPs. In this case they were challenging what they believed to be an injustice.

Case study: Students campaign to stop a deportation

Students from a Plymouth community college started a campaign to stop a family being sent back to Nigeria. Some of the children were attending the school. The family were asylum seekers who had their case to remain in the UK turned down. The family were taken from Devon and held at an Immigration Centre near Bedford. The college students have collected signatures supporting the families case and have over 200 letters of support and are working with their local MP to overturn the decision.

Exam tip

Research through your local media and find examples of citizens working to bring about change locally so that you can write about them in the examination.

How those who wish to bring about change use the media

REVISED

We all now live in a 24/7 news society, where within minutes millions of people know about something happening on the other side of the world. The media – both traditional and the new e-media – is important to those who wish to influence public opinion. It often helps set the political agenda because politicians have to respond when asked or questioned about stories published in the media. Individuals and groups use a range of methods to attract media attention and support.

Groups use a range of ways to gain media coverage. They may publish some authoritative research about any issue, get a celebrity to speak on their behalf, arrange a launch event for a campaign, take some form of action or demonstrate to gain attention. Campaigns may use all of these activities to maintain interest in the issue they are concerned about.

Sometimes the media itself promotes a campaign through programmes or its news. Since 2017, Sky News has promoted the cause of plastic polluting the sea. Sky Ocean Rescue is an example of where the media is leading the campaign (see http://news.sky.com/feature/sky-ocean-rescue-10734494). Both Jamie Oliver and Hugh Fearnley-Whittingstall have in the past promoted change regarding healthy school dinners and changing fishing policy through their television programmes.

The best-known group for their ability to engage with the media were F4J, Fathers for Justice, who were campaigning for better access to their children for fathers who were getting divorced. They staged high-profile stunts, often dressed as characters from comic action books, and scheduled these events around the time the news was broadcast. They notified the media in advance and therefore gained live television coverage, so that millions became aware of their campaign.

In 2003, the Stop the War Coalition organised a demonstration in London to protest against the UK being involved in a war in Iraq.

Demonstrations also took place at the same time in cities across the world. It was the largest demonstration ever seen in London, attracting over 2.3 million people according to some estimates.

Increasingly social media and the internet are playing a bigger role in campaigning. The internet can reach millions within minutes at little cost. Campaigners now gather support, set up petitions and raise funds via the web.

The increased use of social media for political and other campaigning has also led to accusations of groups and others bodies promoting news stories which are distorted and in many cases untrue. This has led to the growth of the use of the term 'fake news' meaning the promotion of stories that are untrue. In recent years the Russian government has been accused of promoting, through non-government bodies, social media stories to bring about political changes it supports in other countries. Many believe that the Russians promoted a pro-Brexit campaign in the UK, supported a pro-Trump vote in the USA and a pro-National Front vote in France.

Exam tip

Remember this changing balance between the power and influence of the traditional media against the power of the internet.

Websites

- 38 Degrees: https://home.38degrees.org.uk/
- Mhairi Black: www.snp.org/mhairi_black – The work of one of our younger MPs
- National Council for Voluntary Organisations: www.ncvo.org.uk – Help understand the scope of voluntary work
- Jamie Oliver Food Foundation: http://jamiesfoodrevolution.org/

Now test yourself

TESTED

1 Define what is meant by a 'pressure group'.
2 Identify one reason for using the internet to campaign.
3 Name the celebrity behind the school dinners campaign.
4 Explain why an organisation may wish to become a charity.

Answers online

Exam practice

The 8-mark question relates to both AO2 and AO3 so you have to apply your understanding and make judgements. The source provides a context but is not intended to directly provide the answer; you should not expect to quote or lift directly from the source and gain marks. The question is about the action of others.

For this sample question please refer to the case study about Grenfell Tower on page 12.
1 Justify the aims you would draft for the local action group mentioned in the source. In your response you should refer to the source and other examples of successful campaigns. [8]

ONLINE

2 Bringing about political change

How citizens can contribute to parliamentary democracy and hold those in power to account

In a liberal democracy, the citizen is seen as being at the heart of political power. The citizen through their vote provides legitimacy to those who win an election. As we live in a representative democracy, the citizen can often appear to be at arm's length from their elected representatives. It is seen as a duty of a citizen in a democracy to take part in the political process to ensure that their voice is heard. By registering to vote and voting at local, national and referendums, a citizen is conferring their legitimacy on our democracy.

Citizens can become more active than just voting at election times. They can join a political party or a pressure group to campaign to bring about change. Through that support and membership they can take part in forms of actions where they seek to influence decision-makers.

Citizens can lobby their representatives to ensure that they are aware of their views. Increasingly, **lobbying** is undertaken using technology rather than a formal meeting in the lobby of the **House of Commons**.

The ultimate power the citizen has in regard to holding those in power to account is how they use their vote at an election. If a citizen feels strongly enough about an issue, they can stand for election.

Lobbying – a campaigning method whereby traditionally members of the public spoke to their MP in the central lobby of the House of Commons to enlist their support for a cause. It is now a generic term used to mean explaining your cause to those you want to influence.

House of Commons – the first chamber of Parliament made up currently of 650 elected members. The government is formed based on the composition of this chamber. It is a legislative chamber that also holds the government to account.

Methods of improving voter engagement and political participation

Traditionally, a citizen would write a letter to a councillor or their Member of Parliament if they wished to raise an issue. One international charity, Amnesty International, developed letter writing into a powerful campaigning tool. A political prisoner would be written to by people from all over the world and the sheer numbers of letters written would often lead to an improvement in their prison treatment or even their release.

Today, people are increasingly turning to digital technology to engage in campaigning about political issues. The government even encourages digital participation through its **e-petitions** website: https://petition.parliament.uk. This system has got checks and balances in that there must be a lot of support for the issue and MPs decide whether it is debated.

Another campaigning group, www.change.org, claims that it achieves victories every day. It claims that over 127 million people have been involved in the campaigns listed on its website. It claims that it has helped achieve 15,387 campaign victories in 196 countries.

E-petitions – a means whereby petitioning can take place online. The government has introduced its own system and many campaign groups have set up their own systems to gather support.

On a personal basis, large numbers of citizens use social media to make their views known about issues, while many celebrities with large followings on social media use it as a campaigning tool. Facebook and Twitter are two of the most used social media formats. David Beckham, for example, has 592,000 followers on Twitter, and has endorsed the work of the children's hospital at Great Ormond Street.

The UK government has its own web pages that promote the idea of volunteering. If you are aged 16 or 17, the government has sponsored the National Citizenship Service programme, which is locally based and involves an element of volunteering. If you prefer to work overseas, the UK government has an International Citizenship Service programme for those aged 18 to 25.

There is also pressure on the government to move faster regarding using digital technology to enhance democracy. It has been suggested that voting be allowed using smartphone technology; government ministers could hold public question time events via social media. Already during elections politicians are keen to use this type of format with bodies like Mumsnet to hold debates (see www.mumsnet.com). The views of the public on issues of the day could be initiated through online referendums.

The issue with many of these suggestions is the role and power of the individual citizen against the role of the elected representative. Giving more power and authority to the individual citizen undermines the power of the elected politician who could become a mere delegate on behalf of the citizens in their area and have to vote or support every issue that achieves majority or the largest minority support.

Action to bring about political change

REVISED

Citizens can take different forms of action to hold those in power to account for their actions. They can do this by:

- joining an interest group or political party
- standing for election
- campaigning
- advocacy
- lobbying
- petitions
- joining a demonstration
- volunteering.

Table 2.1 below needs to be studied alongside Table 1.2 in Chapter 1 (see page 9). The wording for both these elements is almost the same so what is written on page 9 is also applicable for this chapter. Table 2.1 adds a further dimension to this topic by considering examples of the roles undertaken that you may wish to quote in any answer.

The different forms of action citizens can take to hold those in power to account for their actions

This overall statement seeks to bring together all the actions mentioned later in this element, such as standing for election, and these are outlined through examples in Table 2.1.

How the citizen can contribute to public life by joining an interest group or political party

As mentioned in the previous chapter the individual citizen can work with others to bring about change. They can join to act and work locally, join a national group or a group that works on a global basis. Interest groups have a specific interest and only work or promote their own interests. They can be seen as being distinct from campaigning pressure groups that wish to make a difference by promoting an issue or cause and actively campaigning to bring about a change of policy.

Joining a political party means supporting the policies and ideology of that party and working to promote its aims and values. You may decide to campaign on its behalf, raise funds or stand under its banner for elected public office. This could range from standing as a Parish Councillor with a few hundred electors, to a District or County or Unitary Councillor with many thousands of electors, to a directly elected mayor or Police and Crime Commissioner being responsible to several million electors, to becoming an MP/MSP/AM responsible to tens of thousands of electors.

Table 2.1 Examples of actions to bring about political change

Forms of action	Examples
Standing for election	In 2017, Kieron Wilson, 22, a student from Salford University, stood for election in the seat of Bournemouth East as an independent candidate. He wanted to represent the voice of young people in Bournemouth. He outlined plans to set up a volunteer-led mental-health charity, which he would fund partly from his MP's salary. Kieron didn't win a seat at the election but did try to make a difference.
	In 2016, Terence Smith, 19, became the UK's youngest mayor. He was elected as a councillor for Goole, in the East Riding of Yorkshire.

➔

Now test yourself and exam practice answers at **www.hoddereducation.co.uk/myrevisionnotes**

Forms of action	Examples
Campaigning	The UK Youth Parliament is a good example of a body that encourages campaigning by young people (see www.ukyouthparliament.org.uk/campaigns). They chose 'votes for 16- and 17-year-olds in all public elections and referenda' as their national campaign for 2017. Their priority campaign for England was a 'curriculum for life'. A total of 276 Members of Youth Parliament aged 11–18 took part in the debates, the subjects of which were voted for by 978,216 young people across the UK.
Advocacy	UKAN is an advocacy federation that brings together people with a shared interest in mental health (see www.u-kan.co.uk). It is a user controlled national federation of advocacy projects, patients' councils, user forums and self-help and support groups that work in the field of mental health.
Lobbying	Greenpeace is a very successful pressure and lobbying group. On its website it states that decision-makers (like politicians or industry leaders) have both the resources and the responsibility to make positive change happen. 'In our lobbying work, we target and engage those in positions of power and pressure them to take the bold steps needed to protect the planet. We make sure that our campaign demands are clearly heard by decision-makers, and we ask them to translate these demands into real action that protects the environment.' (See www.greenpeace.org.uk/about/how-we-make-change-happen/lobbying.)
Petitions	38 Degrees is a campaigning website that allows people to set up their own petition online (see https://you.38degrees.org.uk). The government also has its own e-petition website (see https://petition.parliament.uk/petitions). The top two e-petitions, with the highest ever number of people signing up to them, are described below: 'We the undersigned call upon HM Government to implement a rule that if the Remain or Leave vote is less than 60% based on a turnout of less than 75% there should be another referendum.' Leave voter Oliver Healey claimed to have set up the petition before the June 2016 referendum, fearing a narrow Remain victory, before it became a de facto protest petition by Remain supporters once the 52–48 majority vote for Brexit was confirmed. In all, 4,150,260 signed the petition. The topic was debated on 5 September 2016 before the government confirmed it would not be pursuing a second referendum. The Foreign Office said: 'The European Union Referendum Act received Royal Assent in December 2015, receiving overwhelming support from Parliament. The Act did not set a threshold for the result or for minimum turnout.' 'Donald Trump should be allowed to enter the UK in his capacity as head of the US Government, but he should not be invited to make an official State Visit because it would cause embarrassment to Her Majesty the Queen.'
Joining a demonstration	In November 2013, a coalition of protest movements, headed by the mysterious 'hacktivist' collective Anonymous, held demonstrations and occupations that have received limited media coverage despite the spectacle of several million people (across 400 cities) donning Guy Fawkes masks to highlight opposition to austerity, extreme inequality and increased state surveillance. Many claim that the Million Mask March is the largest protest ever recorded.
Volunteering	The UK government has its own website for those who want to help others by volunteering (see www.gov.uk/government/get-involved/take-part/volunteer). They state that anyone can volunteer, that it is very rewarding and is a great way to meet new people, gain new or use existing skills, get experience and make a big difference to the community. 'There are lots of easy ways to give your time to help others – from having a cup of tea with an elderly neighbour, to helping out in your local area or making a regular commitment to volunteer with a charity or community group.'

Roles played by groups in providing a voice and support for different groups in society

REVISED

Table 2.2 needs to be studied alongside Table 1.3 (see page 10 in Chapter 1). The wording for this is almost the same so what is written on page 10 is also applicable for this chapter. Table 2.2 adds a further dimension to this topic by considering examples of the roles undertaken that you may wish to quote in any answer.

Human rights – these are basic rights and freedoms to which all people are entitled. Since the end of the Second World War, these rights have been written into a large number of international charters.

Table 2.2 Examples of bodies that provide a voice for different groups in society

Body	An example in helping provide a voice for different groups in society
Public institutions	The Equality and Human Rights Commission (EHRC) is a government-funded quango, which was established by law. Parliament gave the Commission the job of challenging discrimination and protecting **human rights** in the UK. The Commission's work covers the whole of the UK (see www.equalityhumanrights.com). ● Human rights: Promotes understanding of the importance of human rights through teaching, research and public awareness and educational programmes. ● Equality and diversity: Promotes understanding, encourages good practice and promotes equality of opportunity; assistance to victims of discrimination; and works towards the elimination of unlawful discrimination and harassment.
Public services	An ombudsman is a person who has been appointed to look into complaints about companies and organisations. Ombudsmen are independent, free of charge and impartial; that is, they don't take sides with either the person who is complaining or the organisation being complained about. Using an ombudsman is a way of trying to resolve a complaint without going to court. In most cases, the organisation must be complained to first, before making a complaint to the ombudsman. There are a vast number of ombudsmen who cover the public and private sector. The following are examples of public-sector ombudsmen: ● The Parliamentary and Health Service Ombudsman (www.ombudsman.org.uk) investigates complaints about government departments and some other public bodies; they can also look into complaints about NHS hospitals or community health services. ● The Local Government Ombudsman (www.lgo.org.uk) investigates complaints about local councils and some other local organisations.
Interest and pressure groups	Examples of interest groups include the Worldwide Fund for Nature (WWF), Amnesty International, Shelter, the Royal Society for the Protection of Birds (RSPB) and the Electoral Reform Society (described here): *'The Society has thousands of members across the country, an elected council of 15 members and a staff team based in London, Edinburgh and Cardiff. It is an independent campaigning organisation working to champion the rights of voters and to build a better democracy.'* Source: www.electoral-reform.org.uk/campaigns

➜

Body	An example in helping provide a voice for different groups in society
Trade unions	The typical activities of a trade union include providing assistance and services to their members, collectively bargaining for better pay and conditions for all workers, working to improve the quality of public services, political campaigning and industrial action. Nearly 7 million people in the UK belong to a trade union. Union members include nurses, school meals staff, hospital cleaners, professional footballers, shop assistants, teaching assistants, bus drivers, engineers and apprentices. One of the major unions in the UK is UNISON. It has more than 1.3 million members and activists, making it one of Europe's largest unions. More than 70% of its members are women (see www.unison.org.uk/about/what-we-do/about-trade-unions).
Charities and voluntary groups	Citizens Advice is a charity whose work involves a large number of volunteers. It receives funding from the government, among other bodies. In most towns and cities of the UK there are Citizens Advice offices. Many people turn to them to seek help and advice on everyday issues such as housing, benefits entitlements, poverty, legal matters and consumer issues. Citizens Advice works with some of the most disadvantaged in society. Research shows that their clients are five times more likely to live in poverty than the average member of the UK population. Citizens Advice also provides educational services to the general public, and campaigns on social issues (see www.citizensadvice.org.uk).

Websites

- Break the Bag Habit: www.breakthebaghabit.org.uk
- Stop the War Coalition: www.stopwar.org.uk/index.php/about
- Volunteer Match: www.volunteermatch.org
- NCVO: https://www.ncvo.org.uk
- UK government: www.gov.uk/volunteering
- Equality and Human Rights Commission: www.equalityhumanrights.com
- Citizens Advice: www.citizensadvice.org.uk/about-us
- Greenpeace UK: www.greenpeace.org.uk
- Age UK: www.ageuk.org.uk
- The Women's Institute: www.thewi.org.uk

Now test yourself

TESTED

1 Define what is meant by an e-petition.
2 Identify which body you would complain to if you had a problem relating to the work of your local council.
3 Name the government body responsible for dealing with issues relating to discrimination.
4 Explain one benefit of joining a trade union.

Answers online

Exam practice

The 8-mark question relates to both AO2 and AO3 so you have to apply your understanding and make judgements. The source provides a context but is not intended to directly provide the answer; you should not be expected to quote or lift directly from the source and gain marks. The question is about the action of others.

For this sample question please refer to the information about Citizens Advice in Table 2.2.

1 Examine why it is important for a body like Citizens Advice to be independent of the government. In your response you should refer to the source and other examples of the work of voluntary groups. [8]

ONLINE

3 Bringing about change in the legal system

The role of the citizen within the legal system

Citizens take different responsibilities and roles within the legal system, for example as a juror, witness, victim of crime, magistrate, special constable, police commissioner or member of a tribunal hearing.

Central to any justice system within a democracy are the support and involvement of its citizenry. If the citizens of a country had no faith or gave no support to the justice system, it would undermine the concept of living in a democracy. There has been a long tradition of citizen involvement in the justice system in the various parts of the UK. Although you may think first about jury service, which is seen as a civic duty, there are numerous other ways that citizens take part in the justice system as set out in Table 3.1.

Crown Prosecution Service – an independent government body that determines whether charges should be brought. They prosecute cases in the courts on behalf of the state.

Director of Public Prosecutions – the title given to the head of the Crown Prosecution Service (CPS).

Magistrates – part-time community volunteers who after training determine verdicts and sentences in local Magistrates' Courts. They normally sit on a 'bench' of three and jointly agree their decisions.

Special constables – volunteers who help the police on a part-time basis in their local community. They do not have police powers, but they wear a police uniform and assist the police in their community.

Chief constable – the chief police officer within each regional police force responsible for the day-to-day management of police resources to fight crime.

Neighbourhood Watch – a voluntary scheme in which people in a given area work with the police to help reduce crime.

Table 3.1 Ways in which citizens can take part in the justice system

Involvement in the justice system	Commentary
Jury service	Juries are groups of twelve citizens, randomly selected from the local electoral register. They have been shortlisted to hear a case in a court located in their own area. They jointly determine the verdict of the case, making a decision based on the facts and evidence, in consultation with the judge on rules of law. Juries are normally expected to reach a unanimous verdict, but judges can allow them to reach a majority verdict (when one or two jurors disagree with the majority).
A witness	A witness to a crime is vital to the police, the **Crown Prosecution Service** and the defence team of any person accused of an offence. By giving their version of events the witness is able to contribute to the process of justice and perhaps prevent a case of injustice. They may have to appear in court and recount the statement of evidence they have already given. In some very serious cases a witness's anonymity is protected or they are given witness protection.
A victim of crime	It is important if you are a victim of a crime that the matter is reported to the police so an investigation can be undertaken. Once you have reported a crime to the police you have the right to be told about the progress of the case. You are also notified about any arrest and court cases. You should also receive information about victim support, notification about the outcome of the case, information about any entitlement to claim for compensation and support from a family liaison police officer if required.

→

Now test yourself and exam practice answers at **www.hoddereducation.co.uk/myrevisionnotes**

Involvement in the justice system	Commentary
Magistrate	**Magistrates** are also referred to as Justices of the Peace (JPs). They are citizens from the local community who volunteer to administer justice in their local Magistrates' Court. They do not have to have a legal background, as training is provided once they are selected. Advertisements appear in the local press for people to apply to become magistrates. They sit as a 'bench' made up of three magistrates. They can also sit alongside a district judge. All criminal cases start in a Magistrates' Court. Magistrates can give out fines up to £5000 per offence and community orders, and can send an offender to prison for six months, or twelve months for more than one crime. Magistrates have existed for over 600 years. There are currently 30,000 lay magistrates, and almost half are women. Each year about 1600 new magistrates are appointed. When hearing a case, magistrates are supported by a professional legal advisor called the Court Legal Advisor.
Special constable	A **special constable** is a trained volunteer who works with and supports their local police. Special constables can come from any walk of life. They volunteer for a minimum of four hours a week to their local police force. Once they have completed their training, they have the same powers as regular police officers and wear a similar uniform. Traditionally, special constables have not received payment for their work. However, a small number of forces have a system under which special constables are given an allowance in return for specific commitments. The uniform is provided free, and expenses will be paid. In 2015, there were over 16,000 special constables in the UK.
Police and Crime Commissioner	Police and Crime Commissioners are elected posts normally held by candidates who stand under a political label. These are full-time paid posts and their work includes: ● meeting the public to listen to their views about policing ● producing a police and crime plan and setting out police priorities ● deciding how the budget should be spent ● appointing **chief constables** and dismissing them if necessary.
Tribunal member	Citizens can apply to become members of official tribunals, which deal with specific complaints and issues. One of the best known is an Employment Tribunal, which deals with problems relating to work and employment contracts. Tribunals can advertise either for lay members or for those with a specialist background to serve. Local authorities also set up panels to deal with issues like school admission policy and these can invite citizens to become members.
Neighbourhood Watch scheme member	The government and local police forces encourage local residents to work together with them monitoring what is happening in the local community. Many areas have established **Neighbourhood Watch** schemes. Household and motor insurance companies often give discounts to people who live in Neighbourhood Watch areas. People living in an area form a committee and work with their local police force and are encouraged to report any concerns to the police. The police also attend Neighbourhood Watch committee meetings and report back on crime in the area. Together the police and the committee often publish newsletters, so the community is aware of the crime or lack of crime in the area.

Roles played by different groups to bring about legal change or fight an injustice

REVISED

Pressure and interest groups, trade unions, charities and voluntary groups, public institutions and public services all play a role in providing a voice and support for different groups in society campaigning to bring about a legal change or to fight an injustice.

This section follows the pattern established in the earlier two chapters of looking at the context of how different groups can assist the citizen in relation to the content of the theme; in this case Rights and Responsibilities. Table 3.2 uses case studies to show examples of how the various bodies can assist the citizen when campaigning against injustice or for a legal change.

Civil liberties – rights and freedoms that protect an individual citizen from the state. Civil liberties set limits on what a government can do so that it cannot abuse its power or interfere unduly with the lives of private citizens.

Table 3.2 Case studies of legal changes or fighting injustice

Organisation	Case studies of legal changes or fighting injustice
Interest and pressure groups	Liberty is a pressure group that campaigns for **civil liberties** and human rights in the UK (see www.liberty-human-rights.org.uk). It is an independent organisation that tries to hold the powerful to account. Its members have been changing the law since 1934. If you visit their website you will see the range of issues they are currently campaigning about.
	One example of a current issue that Liberty is campaigning on is that soldiers' rights are just as important as civilians', whether they are at home or abroad. For example, soldiers should have the right to train in a safe and supportive environment and have the best available equipment to protect them while doing their job. The Human Rights Act and European Convention on Human Rights (ECHR) protect rights like these. Liberty has helped service people, and their families and civilians, get answers and justice when the Ministry of Defence (MoD) has let them down – from the Snatch Land Rover families to the parents of the young recruits who died at Deepcut barracks.
Trade unions	The Trades Union Congress (TUC) is a high-profile campaigning organisation (see page 10), and health and safety is one of its top campaigning priorities. Trade union campaigns aim to raise awareness of issues in the workplace and put pressure on decision-makers to address these concerns.
	Typical campaigns focus on individual safety issues, defending existing rights and calling for new rights, or national and international days of action. For example, the TUC had a toilet breaks campaign calling for a right for workers not only to have access to a toilet at work but also to have the opportunity to use it (see www.tuc.org.uk/workplace-issues/health-and-safety/campaigns). In July 2017, the Supreme Court ruled in favour of a campaign led by Unison against the introduction by the government of fees regarding Employment Tribunal hearings.
Charities and voluntary groups	The NSPCC is a well-known children's charity. It is also a campaigning organisation on behalf of children's rights. The following is an example of one of their campaigns:
	'Vital changes are needed to ensure young people in the justice system are treated first and foremost as children. Specifically: Young witnesses should have access to a trained communications expert – to help them understand what is happening with the police and court whenever necessary. Children should be able to give their evidence from a location away from court. All judges and lawyers taking child sexual abuse cases should undertake mandatory specialist training.'
	Three months after the NSPCC launched this campaign, the government announced a series of changes to protect vulnerable witnesses in the justice system.
	Other examples of NSPCC campaigns can be found at www.nspcc.org.uk/what-we-do/campaigns).
Public institutions and public services	The Parliamentary and Health Service Ombudsman investigates complaints by members of the public about some public services. In a 2017 report covering a two-month period it upheld 41% of the complaints it investigated. The snapshot contained summaries of 163 investigations, showcasing the wide range of cases the ombudsman service investigates about the NHS in England and UK government departments and their agencies such as the UK Border Force, the Driver and Vehicle Licencing Authority and HM Courts &Tribunals Service. Included in the report are cases about breaches of cancer waiting times, families resorting to putting their family in private care following unsafe discharges from A&E on Christmas Day, people wrongly losing their permanent status to reside in the UK because of poor advice and people going into debt due to incorrect benefit advice. (See www.ombudsman.org.uk/news-and-blog/news/ombudsmans-report-highlights-poor-complaint-handling-and-service-failures-across.)

Exam tip

Remember the specific examples given above do not need to be remembered for the examination. They are just illustrative of different styles and types of campaigning. Do your own local or online research and familiarise yourself with campaigns that interest you.

Different forms of democratic and citizenship actions taken to bring about change and hold those in positions of power to account

There are a number of different forms of democratic and citizenship actions people can take to bring about change and hold those in positions of power to account in regard to issues relating to human rights and the justice system:

- joining an interest group
- campaigning
- advocacy
- lobbying
- petitions
- joining a demonstration
- volunteering.

Again this section is similar to those in the two previous chapters. The emphasis in Table 3.3 will be about how these forms of action have or can be used in regard to human rights and the justice system.

Table 3.3 Case studies relating to human rights and the justice system

Citizen action	Case study regarding human rights and the justice system
Joining an interest group	By joining an interest group you are able to support and promote its campaigns. There are many UK-based groups that campaign in regard to human rights and justice. Some are referenced in this book. The following websites are related to interest groups: • Amnesty International: www.amnesty.org.uk • Humanism: https://humanism.org.uk/campaigns/human-rights-and-equality/ • Justice: https://justice.org.uk/our-work/areas-of-work/ • BIHR: www.bihr.org.uk/about
Campaigning	Campaigning is a generic term that covers a range of methods. In the context of this book it relates to the overarching aims relating to a specific issue. Looking at successful justice campaigns that were citizen led, one of the most prominent has been the Hillsborough campaign for the way in which those involved campaigned for many years, often against the justice system to achieve the outcome they wished. (See www.contrast.org/hillsborough.)
Advocacy	Advocacy is the ability to put forward your point of view about an issue and persuade others. There are also professional advocates, for example those who act on behalf of children in any legal process. Their functions are to: • make sure a child or young person's wishes and feelings are known • attend decision-making meetings with the local authority or school on behalf of a child or young person • uphold a child or young person's legal rights and ensure they are fairly treated • provide impartial information to the child or young person • prepare meetings with social workers for the child or young person • assist the child or young person in making a complaint in a constructive and effective manner • negotiate with social workers and other relevant people • ask questions to relevant people and speak on the child or young person's behalf.
Lobbying	Through lobbying, Amnesty's Internationals UK section and its supporters have exerted significant influence on the UK and devolved governments. This lobbying led to the UK government ratifying the Council of Europe Convention on Action against Trafficking in Human Beings in 2008, and agreed to make women's rights in Afghanistan a priority in 2014–15.

➡

Citizen action	Case study regarding human rights and the justice system
Petitions	Increasingly, citizens are using the internet to indicate their support for causes by signing online petitions. Change.org is a website that allows citizens to generate their own petitions. For example, students at the University of Birmingham have been forced to petition the police after claims a 'drastic' increase in crime has failed to be taken seriously. Within a few days over 4000 people had signed the Change.org appeal after a spate of muggings and burglaries affected those living in the city's Selly Oak area. The petition demands 'increased action and constant police control'. (See www.change.org.)
Demonstrations	In 2002, around 400,000 protesters descended on central London for the Liberty and Livelihood march, which was organised by the Countryside Alliance and aimed to increase awareness of rural issues such as low incomes and poor services, and was opposed to any fox hunting ban. The protesters had travelled from around the country on 2500 coaches and 31 specially chartered trains.
Volunteering	Volunteering can take many forms. An example related to assisting others overseas through giving legal advice is: *'Volunteering on the Law & Human Rights placement in South Africa offers the opportunity to work on really worthwhile projects, alongside likeminded volunteers and passionate staff. Depending on your background, legal knowledge and level of interest in specific areas, you will gain first-hand experience of human rights law in practice, gain knowledge about the legal system as well as learn about community involvement. Volunteers are given the opportunity to get involved at grass roots level, raising awareness about human rights to a variety of people throughout the Western Cape.'* (See www.projects-abroad.co.uk/volunteer-projects/law-and-human-rights/combined-law-and-human-rights/volunteer-south-africa.)

Websites

- Jury service: www.gov.uk/jury-service/overview
- Police Specials: www.policespecials.com
- The Association of Police and Crime Commissioners: www.apccs.police.uk
- Neighbourhood Watch: www.ourwatch.org.uk
- Miscarriages of Justice UK: www.miscarriagesofjustice.org/

Now test yourself

TESTED

1 Define the role of a Police and Crime Commissioner.
2 Identify two ways citizens play an active part in the judicial process.
3 Name a UK-based human rights campaign group.
4 Explain the role of a jury.

Answers online

Exam practice

The 8-mark question relates to both AO2 and AO3 so you have to apply your understanding and make judgements. The source provides a context but is not intended to directly provide the answer; you should not be expected to quote or lift directly from the source and gain marks. The question is about the action of others.

For this sample question please refer to the information about magistrates on page 20.

1 Justify the case for maintaining the current system of lay magistrates. In your response you should refer to the source and other examples of judicial decision-making. [8]

ONLINE

4 About your Investigation

Section A of Paper 1 of the examination is divided into two parts. The first part relates to your understanding of active citizenship. The second part asks questions about the Investigation you have undertaken.

The Investigation is a compulsory part of the course. It is worth 15 per cent of the total marks for the GCSE. You are not able to take any materials relating to your Investigation into the examination. As the choice of title for the Investigation is made by you, there are no set titles or topics. Therefore, the questions on the examination paper have to be of an open style, allowing the response to cover a range of types of Investigation.

There are only four questions about your Investigation; they are worth:
- 2 marks – AO1
- 4 marks – AO2
- 6 marks – AO1 = 2, AO3 = 4
- 12 marks – AO2 = 4, AO3 = 8

The 6- and the 12-mark question are two of three questions in the examination that assess two AOs. The 12 mark question is the highest mark question in the examination. It alone represents 7.5 per cent of the total marks for the GCSE.

To assist you with your Investigation AQA provide a downloadable template on their website (see www.aqa.org.uk) for you to use to be able to make notes about your Investigation and explains the various stages you should follow.

The Investigation falls into three distinct stages:
1 Pre-planning and research
2 Taking action
3 Reflection

Each of these stages is split into two parts. The rest of this chapter follows the structure of the Investigation as set out in the specification. Beside each of the sections are suggested possible questions that could be set. You need to think about how you would answer them in relation to the Investigation you have undertaken.

The first thing you have to do when answering the questions about your Investigation is to briefly outline the nature of your task. This writing doesn't carry any marks but it is important as it allows the examiner to award marks relating to your answers in the context of your Investigation. Ensure that these few sentences clearly show that the Investigation is active citizenship and based upon the specification.

Prior to starting your Investigation

REVISED

You have to decide whether you want to undertake this work alone or with others. Both have benefits and drawbacks and may depend upon the issue you wish to investigate.

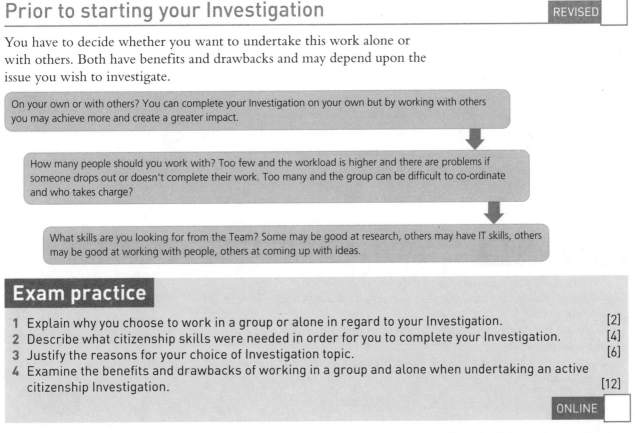

On your own or with others? You can complete your Investigation on your own but by working with others you may achieve more and create a greater impact.

How many people should you work with? Too few and the workload is higher and there are problems if someone drops out or doesn't complete their work. Too many and the group can be difficult to co-ordinate and who takes charge?

What skills are you looking for from the Team? Some may be good at research, others may have IT skills, others may be good at working with people, others at coming up with ideas.

Exam practice

1 Explain why you choose to work in a group or alone in regard to your Investigation. [2]
2 Describe what citizenship skills were needed in order for you to complete your Investigation. [4]
3 Justify the reasons for your choice of Investigation topic. [6]
4 Examine the benefits and drawbacks of working in a group and alone when undertaking an active citizenship Investigation. [12]

ONLINE

Stage 1: The Investigation

REVISED

Look at a copy of the current GCSE Specification and consider any issues that interest you. The issues may be local, national or global or any combination of the three.

A Question is where you are seeking an answer, some information or to raise a doubt about an issue or a problem that needs to be resolved.

A Hypothesis is where you wish to examine and test a theory, proposition or idea. It is used as a starting point for further investigation.

Exam practice

1 Identify the stages you went through from deciding upon the topic that interested you to finalising a question you sought to investigate. [2]
2 Discuss the reasons for your choice of topic and question to investigate. [4]
3 Analyse the benefits of choosing a question that either focuses upon a local issue, a national issue or a global issue. [6]
4 Justify the argument that the question you investigated was clearly based upon the content of the specification. [12]

ONLINE

Stage 2: Carrying out the research

REVISED

Gathering your secondary research materials. Consider the sources that are available to you. Consider issues such as validity, reliability, accuracy, currency and bias.

What primary source information do you need? After reviewing your secondary evidence you may require primary source material and evidence.

Range of evidence and sources. Have you ensured that you have used a range of sources, that are up to date. Evidence that may refute your initial ideas about your Question/Issue should not be disregarded.

The results
What were the results from your secondary and primary research? Are they clear or unclear? Is there a logical progression? Can the results be bunched around key elements of your Question or Issue?

The conclusions
Looking at the results, what conclusions can be drawn? How do these conclusions relate to your Question/Issue. Do your original thoughts about the issue still stand or does the evidence take you in another direction?

Exam practice

1 Identify some primary research that you undertook. [2]
2 Consider the advantages of using primary as against secondary research material in relation to your Investigation. [4]
3 Evaluate the usefulness and place in rank order of importance the evidence you gathered in relation to your issue/question. [6]
4 Examine how the research you undertook impacted upon the wording or direction of your Investigation. [12]

ONLINE

Stage 3: Planning the action

What do we mean by 'taking action'? Presenting a case to others, organising an event, representing the views of others, carrying out a consultation, writing a policy proposal or a review of a policy, setting up an action group. Which is most suited to your Question or Issue?

Create an Action Plan. Break down the Action you wish to take into a sequence of bite size pieces and resolve who is doing what and when they have to complete their task – an Action Plan

Getting approval. Ensure that your teacher has approved your course of action. Ensure you have identified everyone you need to speak to so that any permissions can be sorted out in advance of your action.

Review your planning. Ensure everybody understands what they have to do. If issues arise, have you considered other options? Have you ensured that the action does relate to your Question/Issue and that it can achieve its aims?

Exam practice

1 Explain the course of action that you decided to undertake. [2]
2 Describe the main elements of your plan in relation to your action. [4]
3 Justify why you decided upon the specific action undertaken rather than an alternative form. [6]
4 Justify how your form of action was a form of active citizenship. [12]

ONLINE

Stage 4: Carrying out the action

Reviewing the Action Plan. Is the action plan up to date? Is there a clear line of communication between group members? Is someone in charge and able to make changes if need be?

Have you set your self targets in regard to your action so that you know you have succeeded? Have you ensured that all those outside your group who are involved in the action are aware of their role and have been contacted?

Have you considered how others view your action? Have you built into your action plan gathering data, opinions or views from others about your action? This information will be helpful when you think about evaluating your action.

Exam practice

1 Explain what you hoped to achieve by your action. [2]
2 Describe the targets that you set yourself in order to say your action was successful. [4]
3 Evaluate the usefulness of the evidence/data you gathered to prove your action was successful. [6]
4 Evaluate to what extent your aims for your action were under or over ambitious. [12]

ONLINE

Stage 5: The impact of the action

REVISED

Gathering the evidence
Did you remember to seek others' views about your action? Is this information in a data format that will give you evidence you can use? Has each member of the group written or spoken about their contribution and views?

Successful?
To what extent was your action successful? Did it achieve the aims you set yourselves? Is there evidence to support your view about its degree of success?

Achievement
To what extent did your action make a difference? To what extent did the action relate back to the points raised by your research and your Question/Issue?

Exam practice

1 Identify one measure you used to assess whether your action was successful. [2]
2 Discuss to what extent your action can be considered to be successful or unsuccessful. [4]
3 Examine what further evidence you might have gathered to assess whether your action was successful. [6]
4 Analyse to what extent you can say that your action 'made a difference'. [12]

ONLINE

Stage 6: Evaluating the whole process

REVISED

Reflect
What were the succesful elements of the Investigation?
What things could have been improved?
What is the evidence to support your statements?

In relation to the Question/issue what conclusions did you reach after you had taken the action? Do you feel you made a difference? If so how?

This Investigation enabled you to develop your citizenship knowledge and apply your understanding of citizenship skill, processes and methods to a real life issue of your choice. What have you learnt and/or gained by doing this work?

Exam practice

1 Explain which was the least successful part of your Investigation. [2]
2 Consider: if you were commencing the Investigation again which part of the Investigation would you change and why? [4]
3 Justify which were the most successful elements of your Investigation. [6]
4 Examine how your Investigation enabled you to develop a range of active citizenship skills. [12]

ONLINE

Exam tip

In order to revise for the examination regarding your Investigation use the sample questions in this chapter. Go back to your Investigation document and see if your notes help you answer these questions. If they do not, then when revising add further notes to your Investigation Profile.

5 Political power in the UK

The concept of democracy and different forms of democracy

What does the term democracy mean?

In basic terms, **democracy** is a type of government based upon the principle that all people are equal and collectively hold power. The term derives from the ancient Greek words *demos* meaning people and *kratos* meaning strength/power, hence the link to the expression 'people power'. In ancient Greece, all free men gathered together and debated and decided issues affecting their city-state.

In modern society the term democracy has been broadened to include the following aspects:

- regular, fair and open elections to public bodies
- an electoral system that allows all voters to participate, where there is a secret ballot and an accountable results system, and where the result reflects the views of the electorate
- the ability of citizens to stand for elections without unfair impediment
- a government that is accountable, and faces regular elections
- a system where all candidates can campaign equally and no person can bribe or intimidate to get elected
- a system where the media can freely report upon the work of government
- a system where the judiciary is separate from government and citizens can use the legal process to hold government to account.

These are all elements that have developed over time and are easily recognisable as elements of democracy within the United Kingdom.

> **Democracy** – a system of government based upon the consent of the people through an open and fair electoral system, where electors can choose from competing political parties or groups.

Types of government

Table 5.1 Different types of government

Type of government	Comments
Dictatorship	Rule by one person or group. This person or group is all-powerful. Often associated with a military takeover of a state. Current examples are the leaders of Sudan and Eritrea.
Anarchy	A system where no form of government operates. When there is a total breakdown in society, for example after a civil war, a state of anarchy is said to exist. The country is often divided between power warlords who control militia groups. An example of a country in this position is Libya.
One-party state	A state where only one political party exists and runs the country, and is often associated with a communist form of government, for example North Korea, China, Vietnam and Cuba.
Monarchy	A form of government where political power is held by a family and that power passes down through the generations; hence the term 'absolute monarchy', where all power is held by the monarch. An example of absolute monarchy is Saudi Arabia. The UK is a constitutional monarchy, where almost all of the power normally held by a monarch has been transferred to the elected government.
Theocracy	Where the religious leaders run the country. Iran is an example of a theocracy.

Forms of democracy

Table 5.2 Forms of democracy

Form of democracy	Comments
Liberal democracy	A system of democracy through which certain freedoms of the individual are upheld and citizens are protected from excessive government power. However, the extent of these freedoms and rights can vary from country to country, which equally describe themselves as liberal democracies. The UK and USA and the countries of the EU would describe themselves as liberal democracies.
Direct democracy	A system of government where all citizens take part in decision-making. A modern form of direct democracy is the use of referendums. There has been an increase in the use of referendums in the UK since the first national referendum in 1975 on UK membership of the European Economic Community (EEC), now known as the European Union (EU). A referendum is a vote on a single issue, normally with a YES or NO response required. A national referendum was held in 2016 on the UK's continued membership of the European Union (EU). Since 1998, there have been referendums on Scottish independence, changing the electoral system and the Good Friday Agreement in Northern Ireland.
Representative democracy	A system of government where citizens are elected to represent others in an assembly. UK examples would be: an MP, a councillor or a **Member of the European Parliament (MEP)** elected to serve in the Westminster Parliament, the local chamber and the **European Parliament**, the directly elected Parliament of the European Union.

Issues concerning the way democracy operates within the UK

While the nature of power and the development of democracy in the UK dates from 1215 and the signing of **Magna Carta**, many people feel there are still changes that need to be made to improve the democracy we have in the UK. Table 5.3 sets out some of the issues that arise with the current way democracy operates in the UK.

> **Magna Carta** – known as the Great Charter, signed by King John in 1215. It established the rights and powers of the King and the people of England.

Table 5.3 Issues relating to democracy in the UK

Issue	Commentary
Electoral systems	For differing elections in the UK different voting systems are used. Different voting systems produce different results. Traditionally the UK has used First Past the Post, which means the person who tops the poll wins. Other systems work on a proportional basis where the number of seats won is based upon the percentage of votes gained. Since 1935 no political party has won 50% of the popular vote in a General Election.
Voter turnout	Should a voter be made to vote in an election? In the UK voting is voluntary and often the turnout is very low for local elections. In other countries voting is compulsory and seen as a civic duty. Should we allow voting via the internet to encourage turnout?
Voting age	Currently the voting age in General Elections is 18. In Scotland for some elections it is now 16. At what age should someone be allowed to vote?
Power of politicians	Many countries have fixed-term Parliaments where the date of the next election is known. In the UK the Fixed-term Parliaments Act 2011 fixed the date of future General Elections, but in 2017 the Prime Minister Theresa May arranged with the other parties to call a General Election when she thought she could win. Should politicians have this power?
Unwritten constitution	Unlike many other democracies, the UK has no formal written constitution so Parliament can act as it wishes to do so. Are there sufficient safeguards?

➜

Issue	Commentary
Independence of the judiciary/proactive judiciary	Should the judiciary be given more powers to control decisions made by politicians and Parliament? The **Supreme Court** has some; should they be increased?
Outside interference	Should the UK be subject to decisions by outside bodies? For example, the European Court of Human Rights wanted the UK Parliament to consider giving people in prison the right to vote.
Devolution of power in the UK	Since the late 1990s there has been extensive devolution of power to the nations of the UK. This growth in government sits alongside the existing local government system. Does this extension of democracy develop or undermine the nature of the UK?
Power of the House of Lords	The UK has one of the largest unelected parliamentary bodies in the world. Can a democracy exist alongside a body made up of hereditary peers and political appointees, who have the power to make and amend laws?
Use of direct democracy	In recent years there has been an increase in the use of referendums. Should more decisions be made by the people via referendums? Should e-petitions automatically be discussed in Parliament?

Devolution – the transfer of power from a greater to a lesser body.

House of Lords – the second chamber of the Parliament. Since 1911, it is far less important than the House of Commons. Its main purpose is as a revising chamber. It is made up of non-elected members.

Supreme Court – the final court of appeal in the UK for civil cases, and for criminal cases from England, Wales and Northern Ireland. It hears cases of great public or constitutional importance affecting the whole population.

'Democracy is the worst form of government except all the other forms which have been tried from time to time.'

Sir Winston Churchill, 1947

Exam tip

When considering the way democracy operates in the UK, focus on one or two changes you would support, so you can write in depth instead of just remembering a list.

The values underpinning democracy

REVISED

Within a democratic society there are related **values** as described in Table 5.4.

Table 5.4 Democratic values within society

Democratic value	Definition
Rights	Rights are the legal, social and ethical entitlements that are considered the building blocks of a society. All citizens within our society enjoy them equally.
	The idea of freedom of speech is an essential part of our way of life, but society does limit that right where a right conflicts with other rights. Rights within a society structure the way government operates, the content of laws and the morality of society. Rights are often grouped together and debates take place about human rights, children's rights or prisoner's rights, for example.
Responsibilities	Responsibilities relates to those **duties** placed upon its citizens by a society. For example, you are expected to pay your taxes, obey the law and take part in the judicial system as a jury member if required. These responsibilities are not optional and are often enshrined in law.
Freedoms	Freedom is power or right to speak and act or think as one wants. We often explain freedom in relation to a context. Expressions such as freedom of choice, the freedom of the press and freedom of movement relate to some basic beliefs in our society.

Democratic value	Definition

Equality	Equality relates to how a society treats its members. The concept relates to equal treatment for all. Over the last 100 years there has been a vast number of laws and regulations passed in the UK to ensure equality of treatment and opportunity for all.
	
	The following are examples of legislation relating to equality for differing groups in society:
	● **Rights of women**
	  Representation of the People Act 1928
	  Equal Pay Act 1970
	  Equality Acts 2006 and 2010
	  Sex Discrimination Acts 1975,1986
	  Employment and Equality Regulations 2003 and 2006
	● **Racial equality**
	  Race Relations Acts 1965, 1968, 1976 and 2000
	● **Rights of the child**
	  The United Nations Convention on the Rights of the Child came into force in 1992. Every child in the UK is entitled to over 40 specific rights.
	● **Sexual rights**
	  The Sexual Offences Act 1967
	  Civil Partnerships Act 2005
	  Sexual Offences Act 2003
	  The Gender Recognition Act 2004
	  Marriage (Same Sex Couples) Act 2013
	● **Disability rights**
	  Disability Discrimination Act 1995 and 2005
	  The Special Needs and Disability Act 2001

Values – standards of behaviour that are accepted by a society.

Right – a moral or legal entitlement to have or do something.

Responsibility – the state or fact of having to do something.

Duties – as well as gaining rights as a citizen, states also expect citizens to perform certain duties, for example, in time of war a nation may conscript citizens into the armed forces.

Freedom – the ability to act, speak or think as one wants.

The institutions of the British constitution

REVISED

The institutions of the British constitution are: the power of government, the **Prime Minister** and cabinet; the sovereignty of Parliament; the roles of the **legislature**, the opposition, political parties, the monarch, citizens, the judiciary, the police and the **Civil Service**.

Prime Minister – head of government in the UK; the monarch is Head of State. In the USA, the President holds both posts. The Prime Minister is normally the leader of the largest party in the House of Commons and is an MP. He or she is appointed by the monarch after a General Election. They have the title First Lord of the Treasury.

Legislature – a body normally elected that decides upon the laws that apply to a state. In the UK, Parliament is the legislature; in the USA, Congress is the legislature.

Civil Service – employees of the state who administer our public policy.

Table 5.5 relates to these identified groups and their relationship to the British constitution, for example, how they work and their powers within the context of the UK constitutional and legal framework.

Table 5.5 Elements of the British constitution

Element of the British constitution	Notes	Commentary
The power of government	Within the UK, 'government' is the term given to bodies that make, propose and carry out the policy and laws.	Government is not to be confused with Parliament, which is the sovereign body regarding law-making.
The Prime Minister and cabinet	The Prime Minister is the Head of Government and is normally the leader of the largest party in the House of Commons. The cabinet is formed of the most senior members of the government, appointed by the Prime Minister and members head up government departments like Health and Education. The four most senior members are the Chancellor of the Exchequer, the Foreign Secretary, the Home Secretary and the Minister of Defence.	The Head of State is the monarch. In some systems like the USA, the President holds both posts. There is a concept of cabinet government whereby the Prime Minister is first among equals. The idea is that there is collective decision-making and responsibility. In recent years there has been some growth in the idea of prime ministerial government. Under Tony Blair, the phrase 'sofa government' was used, whereby decision and power seemed to be more centred on the Prime Minister.
The sovereignty of Parliament	This is an important concept. Only Parliament can pass laws in the UK and only Parliament can repeal or change them.	Parliament is sovereign so can pass any laws it wishes. There can be issues when a government has large majorities and stays in power for many years.
The roles of the legislature	The legislature is another name for Parliament, the body that can pass and amend laws. In the case of the UK this can be done through the House of Commons or the House of Lords. The Scottish Parliament also has the ability to pass legislation relating to some Scottish matters.	It can be questioned whether the legislature or the government is most powerful, as governments with large majorities can normally pass all their legislation with ease. The unelected House of Lords often acts as a check on a powerful government as its members are appointed for life and are not accountable like elected MPs.
The opposition	The title 'official opposition' is given to the largest party not in government. It sits opposite the government in the House of Commons. The word 'opposition' relates all those MPs representing parties not in the government. The role is to hold the government to account for its actions and oppose government policies they disagree with.	If a government has a large majority the power of the opposition is often very limited. After the 2017 General Election no party had a majority so the Conservative-led government was vulnerable to losing votes in the House of Commons if a few of its members abstained or voted against it. This gave the opposition parties leverage over the government.
Political parties	Political plurality in a democratic system means that the electorate has a range of political parties from which to choose at elections. A political party is a group of people who share a common ideology and political beliefs and wishes to win elections in order to carry out their ideas. Political parties can either be UK based or from parts of the UK.	Major political parties in the UK: ● **National *:** Conservative 　　　　　Labour 　　　　　Liberal Democrats 　　　　　Greens 　　　　　UKIP ● **Regional:** Scottish Nationalists 　　　　　Welsh Nationals 　　　　　DUP 　　　　　Sinn Fein** * Most do not contest elections in Northern Ireland. ** Win elections in Northern Ireland but refuse to take their seats in the House of Commons.

Element of the British constitution	Notes	Commentary
The monarch	In the UK the monarch is the Head of State. Over the years the majority of the powers of the monarchy have been transferred to the government. The monarch still signs every new Act of Parliament into law and could refuse to do this. However, no recent monarch has refused. The monarchy in the UK is a constitutional monarchy, that is it works within the law as set out by Parliament.	A change to the monarchy in 2015 was that the monarch will now be the first-born child not the first-born male child.
Citizens	Without citizens there would be no state so citizens can claim to be the most important element of the constitution, but they can also appear to be the least effective part. In the UK citizens elect MPs to determine the government through voting. The recent growth in the use of **referendums** enhances the power of the citizen, for example the 2016 vote on leaving the EU.	In many countries citizens take to the streets to demonstrate and protest against the actions of their government, this can often lead to the downfall of the government. In the UK in 1990 there were street protests across the UK about the introduction of what was called the Poll Tax. This was a major factor in Margaret Thatcher having to resign as Prime Minister. Other major demonstrations have taken place since such as the Stop the War movement and anti Students fees protests neither led to a change in government policy.
The judiciary	This term refers to the senior judges. In the UK the judiciary is separate from government and its members are politically impartial. It is very difficult to remove a judge from office. They form a part of the concept of the separation of powers, where each part is distinct and independent: the monarchy, the legislature and the judiciary.	In some countries like the USA judges are either elected public officials or are known for their political beliefs.
The police	In the UK there are a number of regional police forces, all of which are unarmed. They prevent crime, enforce the law, arrest suspects and gather evidence.	The police in the UK were never intended to be a militia, hence the regional forces and being unarmed. Since 2012 they have been accountable to directly elected Police and Crime Commissioners.
The Civil Service	These are the people employed by government to carry out the policies of government and advise government. The civil service is based upon three core principles: **1** Impartiality: Civil servants serve the Crown not a specific government. They cannot be members of political parties. **2** Anonymity: Civil servants are anonymous individuals who should not be identified or associated with specific policies. **3** Permanence: Civil servants stay in their posts when a government leaves office; they are expected to serve governments irrespective of their composition.	In recent years there has been a growth in the number of political advisers employed by government. These political appointees seem to almost provide a separate policy input from ministers and often come into conflict with the work and advice of civil servants.

Some of these elements are clearly more central and important than others but like a jigsaw puzzle you need all the pieces in order to complete the picture.

The relationships between institutions that form the British constitution

REVISED

The nature of the UK constitution

The UK constitution is described as being **unwritten** and **uncodified.**

Table 5.6 The advantages and disadvantages of the way the UK constitution works

	Comment	Advantages	Disadvantages
Unwritten	There is no single written document that is called the British Constitution. There are constitutional laws and conventions.	This makes changing aspects of constitutional law easy, no different than any other type of law.	Gives power to the government of the day to make any changes it wishes. Other countries like the USA have formal written documents and have laid out ways to make changes that involve each state.
Uncodified	There is a range of documents containing aspects of constitutional arrangements. They are not linked or identified as being constitutional.	It enables changes to be made easily, for example lowering the voting age can be looked at in isolation from, say, changing the parliamentary boundaries.	It enables changes to be made piecemeal that could undermine existing constitutional rights when taken together.

Websites

- Parliament: www.parliament.uk
- Prime Minister's Office: www.gov.uk/government/organisations/prime-ministers-office-10-downing-street
- Ministerial Code: www.gov.uk/government/publications/ministerial-code
- British Library: www.bl.uk/magna-carta

Exam tip

Try to see these elements and how they relate to each other as a jigsaw. Focus on the key concepts and from your understanding of them you can construct your argument.

Now test yourself

TESTED

1 Identify a country with a constitutional monarchy.
2 Explain what the phrase 'unwritten constitution' means.
3 Name the political party that is currently the formal opposition in the House of Commons.
4 Define the difference between direct and representative democracy.

Answers online

Exam practice

The US President

President Trump is both the head of state and head of government in the USA. He is also commander-in-chief of the armed forces and can order American forces into action overseas. He was elected in 2016 by winning the largest number of college votes. This system awards votes based upon the population of each state and the candidate who wins the popular vote in a state takes all the college votes for that state. A few states do award the college vote according to the percentage of votes each candidate receives.

For his four years of office the President is often described as the most important politician in the world. His actions are restrained by the US Constitution, for example no non-born American can be president and you must be 40 years of age to stand for election as president.

1 Compare the position of the President of the United States of America as described in the source with that of a UK Prime Minister. [4]

2 Examine the case made by those who say that the UK should have a formal written constitution to safeguard the rights of citizens. [8]

3* Justify the arguments made in favour of the UK not having judges who are elected or political nominees.
In your answer you should consider:
● how judges are currently appointed in the UK
● the advantages and disadvantages of political judicial appointments. [8]

Remember the * means this is a synoptic question where you have to make connections between different parts of the specification. More information is available online at www.hoddereducation.co.uk/myrevisionnotesdownloads

ONLINE

6 Local and devolved government

The role and structure of elected local government

REVISED

Within the UK, as in most countries of the world, the term government refers to a range of structures that operate within a state. They are usually prefixed by words such as central, national, regional or local. These refer to the geographical reach of the powers of these bodies. These different levels of government are often referred to as **tiers** of government. The best analogy is that of a wedding cake, with tiers of cakes with supporting pillars. Figure 6.1 shows how from your home in a local community government can impact upon your life.

> **Tiers** – another term for levels of government.

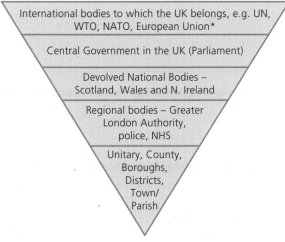

International bodies to which the UK belongs, e.g. UN, WTO, NATO, European Union*

Central Government in the UK (Parliament)

Devolved National Bodies – Scotland, Wales and N. Ireland

Regional bodies – Greater London Authority, police, NHS

Unitary, County, Boroughs, Districts, Town/ Parish

*until the UK leaves the EU in 2019

Figure 6.1 The different tiers of the UK government

There are two important points to remember about local government in the UK:

1 There is no constitutional right for local government to exist. It can be reformed, removed or reshaped at any time at the will of Parliament.
2 The concept of 'ultra vires'. Local councils are only able to carry out the functions allocated to them by **central government**. If they exceed their powers they are 'ultra vires' and any costs involved can be charged to individual councillors who supported the work.

> **Ultra vires** – acting beyond your legal power or authority.
>
> **Central government** – term used to describe the government of the UK.

The role of local government

1 To provide services sanctioned by central government at a local level
2 Part of the democratic process whereby citizens can voice their opinion and stand for elected public office. Provide a platform for the political parties
3 Provide a sounding board to central government on issues of public concern
4 Raise income through various local forms of taxation, such as council tax, parking charges, planning fees, and so on.

5 Promote the well-being of their local community and work with other organs of the state such as the NHS and the private sector, encouraging employment.

6 In many parts of the country they are major employers of professional staff

Structure of local government

Over the years central government has changed the structure of local government, altering the functions they provide, their boundaries, imposing new internal structures and creating new elected roles like that of directly elected mayors. Local government works to a similar pattern in England and Wales; however, Greater London has a different system. Scotland and Northern Ireland have different systems of local government.

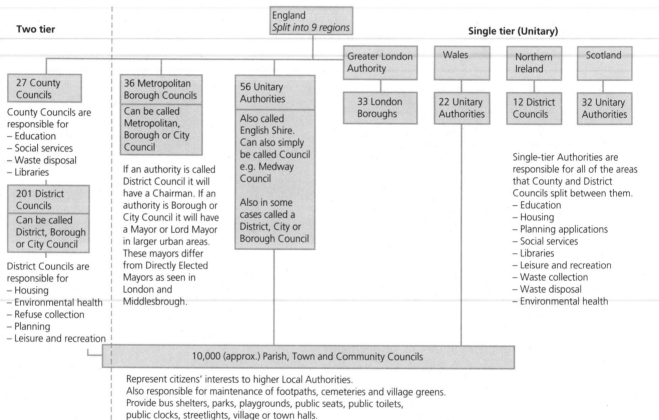

Figure 6.2 The structure of local authorities in the UK

Within the UK there is either one tier or two-tier structure. A single tier structure means there is only one local council providing all the services in a given area. These types of council originated in the cities and urban areas and this is now the preferred model of central government. In 2009 the rural county of Cornwall became a single-tier authority. These types of council are called unitary authorities (one council).

The two-tier model has a number of smaller District Councils within an area of a County Council, each providing different services. London has a two-tier system, the GLA and London Boroughs. Table 6.1 shows which services are provided by each type of local council.

Now test yourself and exam practice answers at www.hoddereducation.co.uk/myrevisionnotes

Table 6.1 What is local government responsible for?

	Unitary authorities	County councils	District councils	Metropolitan districts	London boroughs	Greater London Authority
Education	✔	✔		✔	✔	
Highways	✔	✔		✔	✔	✔
Transport planning	✔	✔		✔	✔	✔
Passenger transport	✔	✔				✔
Social care	✔	✔		✔	✔	
Housing	✔	✔	✔	✔	✔	
Libraries	✔	✔		✔	✔	
Leisure and recreation	✔		✔	✔	✔	
Environmental health	✔		✔	✔	✔	
Waste collection	✔		✔	✔	✔	
Waste disposal	✔	✔		✔	✔	
Planning applications	✔		✔	✔	✔	
Strategic planning	✔	✔		✔	✔	✔
Local tax collection	✔		✔	✔	✔	

Directly elected mayors

For many years central government has encouraged local authorities to have directly elected mayors based on the American model where a single person is in charge of a local authority and works alongside elected councillors. This innovation was often the result of local referendums. Recently the government has further encouraged this move by agreeing to give additional powers to councils that agree to combine and work together and have a directly elected mayor.

On 5 May 2017, six mayors were elected for the first time to lead combined authorities in Cambridgeshire and Peterborough, Greater Manchester, Liverpool City Region, the Tees Valley, the West of England and the West Midlands. The six combined authority areas account for a total population of 9.5 million people, almost 20 per cent of the population in England. The next mayoral elections for the six areas will be held in May 2020.

Exam tip

Research the work of your local council. It is always useful in an answer if you can quote a local example you are familiar with.

How councils operate

Table 6.2 How the councils operate

Way they operate	Comment
Full council	The full council is made up of all elected councillors. The full council debates and decides upon policy based on reports from the various committees.
Committees	Councillors on committees monitor the council's performance and decision-making process and hold it to account for its actions. In councils without a cabinet, these committees have more power as they vote and decide upon council policy.
Cabinet	Like central government where the Prime Minister appoints members of the cabinet who are then responsible for departments (e.g. education), the same concept has been introduced into local government. The party or group that has a majority on the council appoints a leader of the council who works with a small group of councillors who are responsible for a service area. Since 2011, the government has allowed local councils to move back to the old committee system where groups of councillors are responsible for a particular service.

Way they operate	Comment
Leader or directly elected mayor	Traditionally most councils had a mayor as the ceremonial head of the council, normally serving for one year. The party or group with the majority of seats on the council ran the council, appointing one of their members to chair each of the committees, and each party had a group leader on the council. Now councils formally have a leader of the council: the leader of the largest group of councillors or a directly elected mayor who appoints their own cabinet. Many councils still keep the role of a ceremonial mayor. The councillors who accept these more important roles or who are directly elected mayors receive a much higher level of payment than ordinary councillors.

Roles and accountability of local councillors

Table 6.3 Roles and accountability of local councillors

Roles of local councillor	● In many ways local councillors are local versions of your MP. ● They represent the interests of the local community they are elected to serve. ● They represent their political party on the council if they stood under a party label. ● They campaign for the best interests of the whole council area. ● They make representations to other bodies on behalf of their community and the council. ● They hold surgeries in their local areas and deal with issues and problems raised by their constituents. ● They serve on community bodies and represent the council on outside bodies. ● They attend civic and community functions. ● They serve on council committees. ● They help decide on council policy including the level of council tax and its spending plans. ● They hold the council to account for its actions through the ballot box as they face their electorate when they stand for re-election.
Accountability of local councillors	● The local media report on the work of local councillors. ● Section 27 of the Localism Act 2011 requires councils to produce a Code of Conduct for members, to publish the code and indicate the sanctions for members who breech the code. ● Their political party holds them to account for their work as a councillor and can deselect them. ● The financial expenses claimed from the council by councillors are published.

> **Exam tip**
>
> To understand this in more detail, arrange to speak with your local councillor and ask them about their work. You will find a full list of councillors on your local council website.

The nature and organisation of regional and devolved government

REVISED

Devolution is the transfer of power from a greater to a lesser body. In the case of the UK, this relates to the Westminster Parliament agreeing to establish forms of national and regional government. As with the local government system these new bodies have no constitutional right to exist so could at any time be abolished or their power and authority changed. For example, in the case of the Northern Assembly the Westminster government has imposed direct rule from Westminster when power sharing has broken down.

Since 1997, the momentum for devolution in the UK increased. In 1998, a referendum was held and Scotland voted for a Scottish Parliament with the authority to have tax-varying and law-making powers. The Welsh people also voted for an Assembly and power over policy areas. The Good Friday Agreement in Northern Ireland was followed by a referendum in 1998 which re-established **devolved government** in Northern Ireland.

> **Devolved government** – name given to the bodies created under the policy of devolution, such as the Scottish Parliament.

Devolution in the UK created a national Parliament in Scotland, a national Assembly in Wales and a national Assembly in Northern Ireland. This process transferred, and continues to transfer, varying levels of power from the UK Parliament to the UK's nations.

The current political make-up of the three national bodies is shown below. Note the strong representation of nationalist parties in each body. All three bodies have elections based upon differing forms of proportional representation.

Table 6.4 The composition of the three national bodies 2016

Scottish Parliament (129)	Welsh Assembly (60)	Northern Ireland Assembly (89)
Government:	Government:	DUP (28)
SNP (63)	Labour (29)	Sinn Fein (27)
	Liberal Democrats (1)	SDLP (12)
Opposition:	Opposition:	Ulster Unionist Party (10)
Labour (24)	Conservative (11)	Alliance (8)
Conservative (31)	Plaid Cymru (12)	Green (2)
Liberal Democrats (5)	UKIP (7)	Traditional Unionist Voice (1)
Green (6)		Independent (1)

How powers are organised between the Westminster Parliament and the devolved administrations in Northern Ireland, Scotland and Wales

REVISED

Devolved powers are decisions that the UK Parliament controlled in the past, but are now handed over to the devolved bodies, like the Scottish Parliament.

Reserved powers are those still taken by the UK Parliament on behalf of all parts of the United Kingdom: for example, defence and foreign policy.

Each of the devolved bodies has differing powers due to the degree of devolution they were granted by the Westminster Parliament.

- There had been a Northern Ireland Parliament from 1921 until 1972 when direct rule by Westminster was introduced, so it had a tradition of devolved powers.
- Scotland voted in its referendum for a Parliament and tax-raising powers so it has been granted a high degree of devolution and the ability to pass laws.
- The Welsh Assembly was given the least powers, but these have been increased. The majority vote for devolution in Wales was very small.

Table 6.5 Powers devolved to Scotland, Wales and Northern Ireland

Scotland	Wales	Northern Ireland
Agriculture, forestry and fisheries	Agriculture, fisheries, forestry and rural development	Agriculture
Education and training	Ancient monuments and historical buildings	Culture and sport
Environment	Culture	Economic development
Health and social services	Economic development	Education
Housing	Education and training	Employment and skills
Law and order (including the licensing of air weapons)	Environment	Environmental issues, including planning
Local government	Fire and rescue services and promotion of fire safety	Equal opportunities
Sport and the arts	Food	Health and social services
Tourism and economic development	Health and health services	Housing
Transport – many aspects	Highways and transport	Justice and policing
	Housing	Local government
	Local government	Northern Ireland Civil Service
	Public administration	Pensions and child support
	Social welfare	Social security
	Sport and recreation	Transport
	Tourism	
	Town and country planning	
	Water and flood defence	

The position of England

While devolution has been granted to the nations of the United Kingdom some people in England have demanded that there be an English Parliament, while others want regional bodies established. The government has allowed English councils to combine and form regional bodies with directly elected mayors (see pages 39 and 40).

The issue of a parliament is not on the political agenda but the issue of who can vote in Westminster on laws affecting England has now been resolved. It was the case that English MPs could not debate or vote on NHS issues in Scotland because it is a devolved power of the Scottish Parliament, but Scottish MPs could debate and vote on NHS matters in England.

After the 2015 General Election, the Conservative government introduced new stages to the discussion of English-only legislation in an attempt to resolve the 'English votes for English laws' issue. It will be up to the Speaker of the House of Commons to decide when proposed legislation is English only and trigger the new process.

Who can stand for election and how candidates are selected

Standing as a candidate in elections in the UK

Table 6.6 Who can stand for election

Local elections	General Elections
If you want to be a candidate in a **local election** in the UK you must be at least 18 years old, a British citizen, an eligible Commonwealth citizen or a citizen of any other member state of the European Union. You must also meet one of the following four qualifications: 1 You must be a registered elector for the local council area for which you wish to stand. 2 You have occupied as owner or tenant any land or other premises within the local council area for at least twelve months prior to handing in your election nomination papers. 3 Your place of work during the last twelve months is in the local council area. 4 You have lived in the local council area during the whole of the twelve months before the day of your election papers have to be handed in. There are certain people who are disqualified from standing for election: ● if you are employed by the local authority ● if you hold a politically restricted post ● if you are the subject of a bankruptcy restrictions order ● if you have been sentenced to a term of imprisonment of three months or more, including a suspended sentence, during the last five years ● if you have been disqualified under the Representation of the People Act 1983 (which covers corrupt or illegal electoral practices and offences relating to donations).	If you want to become an MP at Westminster, the requirements are: ● you must be at least 18 years old ● you must be either a British citizen, a citizen of the Republic of Ireland or an eligible Commonwealth citizen. There is no requirement in law for you to be a registered elector in the UK. You cannot stand in more than one constituency at the same UK Parliamentary General Election. Citizens of other countries (including EU member states other than the UK, Republic of Ireland, Cyprus and Malta) are not eligible to become a member of the UK Parliament. The following are disqualified from standing: ● civil servants ● members of police forces ● members of the armed forces ● government-nominated directors of commercial companies ● judges ● members of the legislature of any country or territory outside the Commonwealth ● peers who sit in and can vote in the House of Lords ● bishops of the Church of England (known as the **Lords Spiritual**) who are entitled to sit and vote in the House of Lords.

Candidate selection

Each political party has its own methods of selecting candidates and this may vary depending on the type of election a person is being selected for.

When selecting a candidate to stand for a parliamentary election, a local party will advertise in a party journal for those interested to apply. They normally have to be on the list of candidates approved by the national party before they can put their names forward. A selected group of local party workers will draw up a shortlist after interviewing a number of candidates to put to the local party membership. A 'returning officer', a trained member from another local party branch who represents the national party, normally oversees the whole process. The potential candidates are invited to attend a meeting of party members. They address the meeting and answer questions. Through the returning officer they also send a leaflet to all party members asking for their vote. Some parties have experimented with what are called 'open primaries' where any local

> **Local elections** – elections held for councillors to local councils, held on a fixed date in May after the fixed term of office has expired.
>
> **Lords Spiritual** – the 26 bishops of the Church of England who are members of the House of Lords.

resident can vote at a meeting, not just party members. This is often a very expensive exercise. People vote by post or at the meeting and the returning officer is responsible for counting the votes and declaring a winner.

The local party chooses local election candidates. Potential candidates apply and are interviewed and placed on an approved list. If a number of candidates wish to contest a seat, local party members will meet and vote in whomever they wish.

Who can and cannot vote in elections and why; debates about the voting age

REVISED

Local elections

To vote in a local council election you must be on the electoral register and also one of the following:

- of voting age on the day of the election
- a British citizen, a qualifying Commonwealth citizen, or a citizen of the European Union living in the UK.

General Elections

To vote in a UK General Election a person must be registered to vote and also:

- aged 18 or over
- be a British citizen, a qualifying Commonwealth citizen or a citizen of the Republic of Ireland
- not be subject to any legal incapacity to vote.

The following people cannot vote in a UK General Election:

- members of the House of Lords (although they can vote at elections to local authorities, devolved legislatures and the European Parliament)
- EU citizens resident in the UK (although they can vote at elections to local authorities, devolved legislatures and the European Parliament). (This will form a part of the negotiations with the EU following the UK decision to leave the EU in June 2016.)
- anyone other than British, Irish and qualifying Commonwealth citizens
- convicted persons in prison, though remand prisoners (unconvicted prisoners) can vote if they are on the electoral register
- anyone found guilty within the previous five years of corrupt or illegal practices in connection with an election
- if you have been detained under certain sections of the Mental Health Act.

In England, Northern Ireland and Wales, you can register to vote when you are 17. However, you can only vote when you are 18. In Scotland, you can register to vote when you are 15. You can vote in local and Scottish Parliament elections when you are 16 and UK Parliamentary and European Parliamentary elections when you are 18.

The debate about the voting age

During the twentieth century, there were many debates about who could vote and at what age. Women were first given the vote in General Elections in 1918, but they had to be 30 years old. Men could vote at 21. In 1928, women were given the vote at 21.

Lowering the age of voting

In 1970, the voting age was lowered to 18. In the 2014 referendum on Scottish independence the voting age was 16. In Scotland 16-year-olds are allowed to vote in elections to their councils and Parliament. Many people now argue that the voting age should be lowered to 16 for all parts of the UK and all elections. Many of the major political parties support the lowering of the voting age to 16.

> **Exam tip**
>
> Remember when writing about issues such as lowering the voting age there is no right or wrong answer, all you need do is justify your point of view with evidence.

Issues relating to voter turnout, voter apathy and suggestions for increasing voter turnout at elections

REVISED

For a number of years, politicians have been concerned about the turnout at various elections in the UK. This was one of the factors behind introducing Citizenship as a National Curriculum subject in schools. **Voter turnout** refers to the number of people who vote as a percentage of the number of people who could vote. There is also the factor of people not registering to vote. Many argue that this lack of turnout is due to **voter apathy**; people not being interested in politics. But the counter-argument is that many get involved in the political process in other ways, for example pressure groups and campaigns.

> **Voter turnout** – the percentage of voters who actually vote against the total number who are registered to vote.
>
> **Voter apathy** – a lack of interest by citizens in the electoral and political process.

Table 6.7 Turnouts in different elections

Year	Type of election	(%) turnout	Year	Type of election	(%) turnout
2009	European	34.7	2011	Northern Ireland Assembly	54.7
2009	Local election average	39.2	2012	London Mayor	37.4
2010	General Election	65.1	2012	Local average	31.3
2011	Local election average	42.6	2012	Police and Crime Commissioners	15.0
2011	Welsh Assembly	41.5	2014	Referendum on Scottish Independence	84.6
2011	Scottish Parliament	50.4	2016	EU Referendum	72.0
			2017	General Election	68.7

One of the major concerns regarding voter apathy is about young people aged 18–25 not bothering to vote. Interestingly in the 2017 General Election young people turned out to vote in higher numbers than in past elections. Figures 6.3 and 6.4 indicate the turnout by age in the 2017 General Election and how people voted by age in the same election.

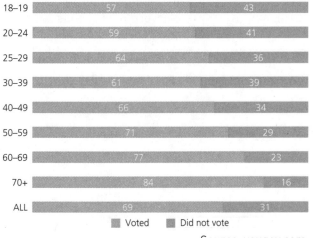

Source: yougov.com

Figure 6.3 Turnout by age in the 2017 General Election (based on a survey of 52,615 UK adults)

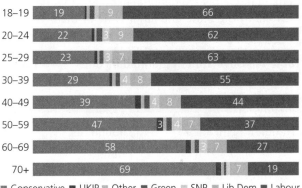

Source: yougov.com

Figure 6.4 How people voted by age in the 2017 General Election (based on a survey of 52,615 UK adults)

Suggestions for improving voter turnout

The **Electoral Commission**, the government body responsible for the running of elections, has published reports looking at changes that might encourage more people to vote. A number have been tried out in some local elections. These include:

- allowing weekend voting
- changing polling hours
- opening polling stations in different locations
- encouraging postal voting and early voting.

Others have suggested online voting or telephone voting. These are all system changes to get people more interested and involved in politics. But is it politics and the way we do politics that has to change? Some would suggest changing the voting system, allowing for a re-call of MPs to make them face re-election, making more use of local referendums, and ensuring that more e-petitions are discussed and acted upon by Parliament, or even making voting compulsory as in countries like Australia.

> **Electoral Commission** – a government-established body that monitors and oversees all UK elections and referendums.

> **Exam tip**
>
> When writing about elections or voting remember to use contemporary evidence, not material from 50 or 100 years ago.

How public taxes are raised and spent by government locally and nationally

REVISED

Tables 6.8 and 6.9 indicate the government planned income and spending for 2017–18. These figures are updated annually when the Chancellor of the Exchequer introduces the annual **Budget**. The tax year starts on 6 April each year. The UK economy is called a mixed economy; it is one of several different ways the economic system of a country can be defined, see box below.

> **Command economy** – a national economy where all elements of the economic system are controlled by the government.
>
> **Market economy** – a national economy where most of the economy is run by the private sector and the state owns and runs limited elements.
>
> **Mixed economy** – a national economy that has elements run and owned by the state and others run by the private sector.

> **Budget** – an annual statement made by the Chancellor of the Exchequer to the House of Commons about the taxation and spending policy for the forthcoming year.
>
> **Nationalised** – where the state owns and runs a part of the economy.
>
> **Real government spending** – the change in the amount a government spends after taking account of inflation.

Table 6.8 Government planned income for 2017–18

Income tax	£175bn
National Insurance	£130bn
Excise duties	£48bn
Corporation tax	£52bn
VAT	£143bn
Business rates	£30bn
Council tax	£32bn
Other (taxes)	£80bn
Other (non-taxes)	£54bn

Source: Office for Budget Responsibility 2017–18

Table 6.9 Government planned spending for 2017–18

Social protection	£245bn
Personal and social services	£32bn
Health	£149bn
Transport	£37bn
Education	£102bn
Defence	£48bn
Industry, agriculture and employment	£23bn
Housing and environment	£36bn
Public order and safety	£34bn
Other including EU transactions	£50bn
Debt interest	£46bn

Source: Office for Budget Responsibility 2017–18

Table 6.10 Government income and spending

Government income	Government spending
The three largest sources are: ● **Income tax** – paid by everyone earning or having an investment or savings income above a set annual level ● **National Insurance** – paid by everyone aged below 65, in employment, earning above a set level ● **Value-added tax (VAT)** – paid on a large range of goods and services; excise duties relate to additional duties on items such as alcohol. Other sources of government revenue include: **Corporation tax** is paid by companies on their profits. **Business rates** are paid by businesses based on the value of their properties.	Once a government has a spending programme, it must agree how to raise the money to pay for the services it wishes to provide. It can do this through taxation or by increasing its debts. **Welfare-related spending** – areas such as personal social services, health, education and social protection account for a very large part of government spending. **Debt interest** – this relates to the interest the government pays on the national debt, which has accumulated over several hundred years.

Local government income

Council tax is the annual tax levied by local councils on properties in their local area. Local authorities have limited room for raising income because the bulk of their income comes from central government grants. The amount of money raised by council tax is often subject to government pressure to be kept low. The rest of local government income comes from charges they make for their services. Local government spending relates to the services shown on page 46.

> **Exam tip**
>
> When discussing figures like those from the budget you don't need to know the figure to the nearest million, you can write 'more than £400 million' or 'several billion'.

Budgeting and managing risk and how government manages decisions about the allocation of public funding

REVISED

Party policy

The government uses a variety of measures to decide its spending priorities. The initial decisions will be based upon the political philosophy of the party in government and whether it is in favour of higher or lower government spending. It would have made certain commitments in its **manifesto** at the General Election, so will feel it has to deliver on its political promises.

> **Manifesto** – a document produced by a political party at the time of an election outlining the policies it would like to introduce.

UK economic issues

Some decisions will relate to economic factors, such as encouraging economic growth, lowering unemployment and bringing more people back into the workforce. These policies might then have an impact on welfare policy, such as the provision of childcare. Policies in relation to education might relate to improving the skills make-up of the future workforce or increasing university participation.

Long-term issues

Some issues will relate to long-term government spending, such as reviewing pension ages and entitlements and dealing with an ageing population in terms of care and health service provision.

Events when in office

Other issues will emerge once a government is in office and require almost instant decisions about government spending: for example, the

Grenfell Tower fire in 2017 will lead to money having to be spent by council and social housing providers. It may also cause a long-term review of the provision of social housing throughout the UK.

Irrespective of which party or parties are in power, these issues all need to be considered. If the economy is growing it is easier for the state to spend more money and actually take a lower percentage of the nation's **Gross Domestic Product (GDP)** in taxation at the same time.

> **Gross Domestic Product (GDP)** – the value of all the goods and services created in a country, normally measured on an annual basis.

Governments have three options if they wish to increase government spending.

1 Increase taxation to generate more government income
2 Borrow additional money, thereby increasing the government debt
3 Make assumptions about economic growth which will lead to existing taxes raising more income

Problems arise when there is a crisis or economic growth stops or goes into reverse. A government is then trapped by greater demands for its services due to increased unemployment and lower spending in the economy, cutting its tax revenues. It can also be committed to maintaining the existing levels of provision which may have become more generous during the years of growth.

In 2015, the government launched an independent National Infrastructure Commission to oversee its £100 billion spending on infrastructure planning. The money will be spent by 2020 on 'vital projects', such as road, rail and flood defence improvements. The Commission will focus on three particular areas: connections between cities in the North, London's transport system, and energy. It is charged with producing a report at the beginning of each Parliament, providing recommendations for spending on infrastructure projects.

Debates about how governments and other service providers make provision for welfare, health, the elderly and education

REVISED

Table 6.11 shows a case study in regard to each topic. The differing viewpoints represent a range of points of views across the political spectrum. You need to consider which viewpoint you support and whether you can provide sufficient evidence to support your point of view.

> **Inflation** – the rate at which prices and wages increase on an annual basis.

Table 6.11 Viewpoints on service provisions

Service provision	Case study	Differing viewpoints
Welfare benefits	The overall benefit bill needs to be kept restrained and people should be encouraged back to work; it shouldn't pay to live off welfare benefits against going to work.	• The state should provide a basic income to allow those in need to live a normal life. • By cutting back on welfare payments claimants are encouraged to go out and look for work.
Health	The National Health Service needs increased funding. It has been suggested by one political party that the NHS and social care be funded through a separate tax so people are aware of how much it costs and that NHS spending should be independently decided.	• The state should involve a range of providers for NHS services so they promote competition and enable the service to become more efficient. • The NHS should be funded from general taxation and it should be given additional money every year to maintain and improve services. It should remain free of charge at the point of delivery for everyone.

➜

Service provision	Case study	Differing viewpoints
Elderly people	Old-age pensions are currently decided through a triple lock provision, whereby pensioners receive the higher figure of wage **inflation**, CPI (price inflation) or 2.5%. One political party has suggested that the 2.5% part of the lock be removed.	• The triple lock provides some security for the poorest and most vulnerable in society. 2.5% is the least they deserve each year. • In recent years the triple lock has protected pensioners' income; it is now time to help others in society.
Education	Each school in the country is currently funded on a formula that has not been changed for many years. The government has proposed changing the formula to treat schools more equally. Some schools will gain while others will lose out on funding.	• The system must be made fairer but within the existing budget allocation, so there will be winners and losers. • We need to invest more money in our schools to improve pupil outcomes in order to provide the skilled workforce for tomorrow.

Websites

- Local Government Association: www.local.gov.uk
- The Electoral Commission: www.electoralcommission.org.uk
- UK Parliament: www.parliament.uk
- Scottish Parliament: www.parliament.scot/
- Welsh Assembly: www.assembly.wales/en/Pages/Home.aspx
- Northern Ireland Assembly: www.niassembly.gov.uk
- Greater London Authority: www.london.gov.uk
- UK government: www.gov.uk

Now test yourself

TESTED

1 Explain one role of an elected local councillor.
2 Identify which part of the UK has its own national Parliament.
3 Explain what is meant by the term 'devolution'.
4 Name the body that oversees the running of elections and referendums in the UK.

Answers online

Exam practice

1 Using Table 6.5 on page 42, discuss why some elections have a higher turnout than others. [4]
2 Justify a case for raising taxation in order to spend more money on the National Health Service. [8]
3* Many people say their vote doesn't count or is a wasted vote as the party they vote for never wins the seat.
   Justify a case that says that changing the voting system for electing MPs would increase voter turnout and decrease voter apathy.
   In your answer you should consider:
   - the range of voting systems available
   - how to end voter apathy and increase voter turnout. [8]

ONLINE

7 Where does political power reside?

The nature of the 'First Past the Post' system and the frequency of Westminster elections

The United Kingdom is a representative democracy where approximately every five years the electorate votes and elects a new Parliament, currently comprising 650 MPs. There are proposals to reduce this number to 600.

A constituency

Every MP represents a **constituency**, which is geographical area made up of about 68,000 electors. Some electorates are smaller and others larger. Again it is proposed when the number of MPs is reduced to make almost all constituencies have a similar electorate. Each constituency elects one MP using the **first past the post (FPTP)** election system.

> **Constituencies** – a named geographical area consisting on average of about 65,000 voters which elects a single MP to the UK Parliament.
>
> **First past the post** – an election system based upon the candidate with the highest number of votes cast being elected.

Date of the election

By tradition General Elections are held on Thursdays. Up until 2010, it was up to the Prime Minister to decide the date of the next election, unless they were forced into calling an election by a vote of no confidence in the House of Commons (this happened in 1979). The Fixed-term Parliament Act 2012 set a five-year fixed term for Parliament unless a two-thirds majority of MPs voted for an election; this happened in 2017.

How does the system work?

Each voter who is registered on the electoral register votes by either:
- going to a polling station
- voting by post
- having a proxy vote whereby someone votes on their behalf.

Each voter is given a ballot paper and places an X against the candidate of their choice and then places their vote in a ballot box. When the votes are counted the candidate with the most votes is elected.

A by-election

When an MP dies or resigns, a by-election is called. The seat is not left vacant until the next General Election but an election is held in that seat to elect a new MP.

2017 General Election Results

Table 7.1 Votes received for each of the major parties

Party	Total vote (millions)	%
Conservatives	13.7	42.5
Labour	12.9	40.0
Liberal Democrats	2.8	7.4
SNP (votes only from Scotland)	0.9	3.0
UKIP	0.6	1.8
Greens	0.5	1.6

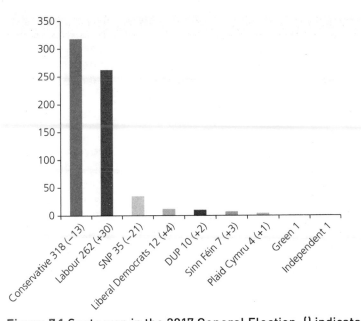

Figure 7.1 Seats won in the 2017 General Election. () indicates the change in number of MP's since the 2015 General Election

Advantages and disadvantages of other voting systems used in UK elections, including proportional systems

REVISED

As well as FPTP, a range of other systems is used for different elections in the UK. Voting systems fall into two types: **proportional** and non-proportional.

- **Proportional systems** – the number of votes given to a party at an election is reflected in the number of people elected. For example, if the House of Commons had 600 members and the Greens got 10 per cent of the vote they would expect to have 60 MPs.
- **Non-proportional** systems like FPTP rely on gaining the most votes in an individual constituency to win, so there is no link between the national vote for a party and the number of MPs elected.

Proportional – a system of voting whereby the number of people elected relates to the number (percentage) of votes cast.

Table 7.2 Other voting systems

Name of system	Where it is used	Description	Advantages	Disadvantages
Closed Party List	European Parliament	Voters cast a single vote for a party on a party list. The number of votes gained by the party determines how many of their members are elected.	This system lends itself to greater proportionality than others.	The voter has no choice regarding the order of the candidates on the party list.
First Past the Post (FPTP)	UK Parliament	The candidate with the most votes wins. A non-proportional system. A referendum was held in May 2012 to change the way we elect MPs to the AV system. The proposal was rejected.	This system is simple to use. The outcome is quickly known.	People can be elected on a minority of the vote. Governments are elected on a minority of the vote. Smaller parties are under-represented.
	Local authority elections in England and Wales	Councils can choose to call an election every three years, or a third to retire each year. County councillors are elected every four years.		

Name of system	Where it is used	Description	Advantages	Disadvantages
Single Transferrable Vote (STV)	European Parliament (Northern Ireland) Northern Ireland Assembly Northern Ireland local councils Scottish local councils	Proportional system where the electors place candidates in number order. Each candidate must achieve a quota of votes to win. Votes above the quota are redistributed to the voters' lower choices.	Every vote does help elect someone. The result closely matches the vote cast for each party.	This system often leads to many parties electing candidates. Coalition governments are more likely. Results can take time to count.
Supplementary vote (SV)	Directly elected mayors Police and Crime Commissioners	Voters have a first and second choice candidate. The winner must receive over 50% of the votes. Lowest scoring candidates are elected and their second votes redistributed.	Ensures that the winner has over 50% of the votes cast.	Often the winner relies on others' second choices.
Additional Member System (AMS)	Scottish Parliament Welsh Assembly Greater London Authority	Voters have two votes, one for a candidate and the second for a party list. The first votes operate as a FPTP system and the second act as a top-up vote to ensure that the overall vote is proportional when additional members are elected from the party list.	Ensures that the wishes of the voters are more closely aligned to the outcome.	Ends up with two types of elected member – one directly elected and another from a list.

Exam tip

Start revising this section by being clear about the two types of voting systems; proportional and non-proportional. Try to revise how one of each works.

Supplementary vote – a voting system used in the UK where voters have a second vote which is used in the election process if no candidate gets 50 per cent of the first-choice votes.

REVISED

The difference between the executive, the legislature, the judiciary and the monarchy

This section of the course relates to the different elements and ideas that make up how Parliament works.

Table 7.3 The separation of powers in the UK

Element	Commentary
The Executive	The executive is the branch of government made up of the Prime Minister and other ministers, senior civil servants and policy advisors who draft and then, in the case of the civil service, implement the policy after it has been agreed by the legislature.
The Legislature	The legislature is the body that makes law. In the case of the UK it is Parliament sitting in Westminster, made up of the House of Commons and the House of Lords.
The judiciary	The judiciary comprises the judges and the legal process. Decisions made by government ministers and by Parliament can be challenged in court and often legislation can be interpreted, so judges have to make a determination regarding its meaning. While the judiciary is supposed to be separate and independent of the other two elements, it can become 'political' by the decisions it makes. If the government does not like the interruption by the judges or the way the law has been interpreted, it can review the situation and draft new laws or regulations to achieve what was originally intended.

→

Element	Commentary
The monarchy	The UK is a constitutional monarchy and citizens of the UK are subjects of the monarch. The role of the monarchy today is largely ceremonial. Monarchy is a traditional form of government whereby power is passed down through the family line. Over hundreds of years the power of the monarchy has been transferred to the elected government. Some countries still have a system of government based upon the monarch having absolute power.
	The monarch appoints a Prime Minister after each General Election. The monarch each year formally opens Parliament and reads the Queen's Speech. It is actually written by the government and sets out its legislative programme for the next twelve months. The monarch formally dissolves Parliament before a General Election. When a bill is passed by Parliament, the monarch formally agrees it – this is when it is given Royal Assent. This changes a bill into an Act of Parliament, making it a law.
Bicameral parliament	In the UK, Parliament is made up of two parts: the House of Commons and the House of Lords. This system of a two-chamber legislature/parliament is called bicameral (two chambers). It is a pattern followed in many other countries: for example, the Congress (Parliament) of the USA is made up of the House of Representatives and the Senate.
House of Commons	This is an elected chamber currently made up of 650 members. The government is formed on the basis of elections to this chamber. The Prime Minister and most government ministers are members of this House. From a government's perspective, the main function of the House of Commons is to vote the policy of the government into legislation. The will of the House of Commons is always supreme. The Commons sees its role as holding the government to account for its actions, debating and amending bills and being a forum for national debate.
House of Lords	The House of Lords is made up of over 1000 appointed life peers and some hereditary peers and bishops of the Church of England. The role of the House of Lords is to debate and revise legislation from the House of Commons. It can also propose legislation (normally about uncontroversial issues) and it carries out scrutiny functions similar to the House of Commons. At times, there are joint committees of both Houses. The House of Lords does not vote down proposals from the government if they were in its election manifesto.

The major political parties contesting UK General Elections

REVISED

Brief historical background to UK political parties

- The party-political system we have in the UK dates back to the mid-nineteenth century, when the political divide was between Whigs and Tories.
- After the mid-1800s, these two informal groups became established national political parties; the Liberals and the Conservatives.
- At the turn of the twentieth century, a third party emerged established by the trade union movement: the Labour Party.
- After the First World War, the Liberals went into decline and a **two-party system** emerged made up of the Conservative and Labour parties.
- From the mid-1970s onwards the make-up of Parliament began to involve a wider range of parties including the Scottish and Welsh Nationalists and a number of parties from Northern Ireland. The Liberal Party merged with the SDP, a party made up of MPs who had defected from the Labour Party in the early 1980s, to form what has become the Liberal Democrats. More recently the Greens have emerged as a national force as have UKIP (the United Kingdom Independence Party).

> **Exam tip**
>
> Parliament is the institution, the Palace of Westminster is the building. It comprises two parts – the House of Lords and the House of Commons – and the Commons is the all-powerful part.

> **Two-party system** – a political system that is dominated by two political parties, each of which may at some time form a government

● The 2017 General Election saw a return to a clear two–party system where the Conservatives and Labour between them took over 80 per cent of the vote.

Political ideology

Political parties are distinguished from each other by their political ideas and policies; the term ideology means a group of connected political ideas that form a coherent set of values that underpins the way a political party considers any political issue. Traditionally political parties have been labelled as being to the right, left or centre.

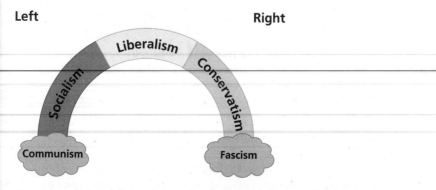

Figure 7.2 Parties are traditionally described as right, left or centre

The political ideologies associated with the main UK political parties are:
● Socialism – associated with the Labour Party, based on common ownership, a belief in community and equality. It ranges from communism to social democracy.
● Conservatism – associated with the Conservative Party, based upon tradition, duty and authority and property. It encompasses views from Tory paternalism to the **New Right**.
● Liberalism – associated with the Liberal Democrats that is concerned about human rights and **individual liberty**, freedom and **tolerance** and consent. Modern liberalism differs from classical liberalism due to a greater emphasis on social and welfare issues.

Some of the policy ideas set out in the main parties' manifestos at the 2017 General Election can be seen in Table 7.4.

> **New Right** – a view of conservatism, linked to Ronald Reagan in the USA and Margaret Thatcher in the UK in the 1980s, that limiting the impact of the state on business and lowering taxation and what services the state provided was the best means of increasing national wealth and allowed for personal empowerment and increased social mobility.
>
> **Individual liberty** – the concept that in a modern democracy people have the freedom to make their own choices and decisions.
>
> **Tolerance** – a concept based upon the idea that in a modern society people show understanding of others with differing views and opinions.

Table 7.4 Some policy ideas at the 2017 General Election

Policy area	Conservatives	Labour	Liberal Democrats
Education	● Increase the overall schools budget in England by £4bn by 2022 ● No school will have its budget cut as a result of the new funding formula ● End the ban on new selective schools ● Introduce T-Levels	● Abolish university tuition fees and reintroduce maintenance grants ● 30 hours of free childcare for two-year-olds in England ● End the public sector pay cap for teachers ● Restrict primary class sizes to 30 and introduce free school meals for primary school children	● Spend £7bn extra on education, increasing school budgets and the Pupil Premium ● Oppose grammar schools ● End the 1% cap on teachers' pay rises ● Reinstate maintenance grants for the poorest students

→

Policy area	Conservatives	Labour	Liberal Democrats
Health	• £8bn increase to NHS England budget compared to current level by 2022–23 • Include value of family home in means test for people receiving social care at home • Cost of care to be capped and people guaranteed to keep £100,000 of assets once care bill paid • Allow deferral of care bills until after death to ensure no one is forced to sell family home	• Commit to more than £30bn in extra funding for the NHS in England over the next five years • Reverse privatisation and return health services into public control • Guarantee access to NHS treatment within 18 weeks and A&E within four hours • Lay the foundations of a National Care service and put an extra £8bn into social care over the next five years	• Add 1p onto each rate of income tax and ring-fence the money for NHS and social care • Ensure mental health care waiting time standards match those in physical health care • Ensure that there are more nurses on hospital wards and in the community • Introduce a Welsh NHS whistle-blowing hotline
Economy	• Achieve a balanced budget by 2025 • Rule out increases to VAT • Stick with current plans to raise personal tax allowances and cut corporation tax • Review the business rates system	• Introduce a £250bn stimulus package over ten years • No increases in personal National Insurance or VAT • Reintroduce a 50p tax rate and raise income tax for those who earn over £80,000 • Raise corporation tax rates to 26% by 2020–21	• Balance day-to-day spending while reducing national debt as a proportion of GDP • Add 1p onto each rate of income tax and ring-fence the money for NHS and social care • Borrow £100bn to invest in infrastructure, including housebuilding, broadband, schools, hospitals and transport • Reverse some planned cuts to corporation tax, capital gains tax and inheritance tax
Transport	• Invest £40bn across the rest of this decade on transport improvements • Work with train companies and employees to agree to minimum service levels during industrial disputes • Expand Heathrow airport • Remove the 'complexity and perverse pricing' of rail tickets	• Renationalise Britain's railways as franchises expire • Let local councils take over bus services if they wish to • New clean air act to legislate against diesel fumes • Ban fracking	• Introduce a diesel scrappage scheme • Extend ultra-low emission zones to ten more towns and cities • Set legally binding target of zero net greenhouse gas emissions by 2050 • Oppose fracking

→

Policy area	Conservatives	Labour	Liberal Democrats
Brexit	• Leave the single market and customs union, while seeking a 'deep and special partnership' with the EU • Secure a 'smooth and orderly Brexit' while maintaining that 'no deal is better than a bad deal for the UK' • Determine a 'fair settlement of the UK's rights and obligations' in our withdrawal from the EU • Pass a Great Repeal Bill to convert EU law into UK law	• Scrap the Brexit white paper and replace it with a fresh set of negotiating priorities with an 'emphasis on the single market and customs union' • Immediately guarantee rights of EU citizens living in Britain • Replace the 'Great Repeal Bill' with an EU rights and protections bill that will ensure no change to workers' rights or environmental protections • Reject 'no deal' with the European Union as a viable option	• Hold a referendum on the final Brexit deal, with the option to remain in the EU • Unilaterally guarantee the rights of EU nationals in the UK • Stay in the single market and customs union • Support the principle of freedom of movement between the UK and EU – the right to work, travel, study and retire abroad
Immigration	• Reduce net migration to tens of thousands • Double the Immigration Skills Charge on companies employing migrant workers • Increase minimum earnings threshold for family visa sponsorship • Toughen requirements for student visas and rules allowing them to stay and work	• Freedom of movement will end when Britain leaves the European Union • Reinstate the Migrant Impact fund in areas where immigration has placed a strain on public services • Take students out of immigration numbers • Recruit 500 more border guards	• Support the principle of freedom of movement between the UK and EU • Allow high-skilled immigration to support key sectors of the economy • Remove students from official migration statistics • Welcome 50,000 Syrian refugees over five years and re-establish the 'Dubs' child refugee scheme

> **Exam tip**
>
> To keep up to date regarding party policy always visit each party's website.

Brexit – British withdrawal from the European Union (British exit).

How Parliament works: scrutinising government and making it accountable

Parliament works by holding the government to account for its actions in several ways: questioning, the committee structure and debates, as shown in Table 7.5.

Table 7.5 Ways in which Parliament can hold the government to account

Parliamentary accountability	Commentary
Questions	Members of Parliament – both in the Commons and the Lords – are able to ask ministers or the Prime Minister questions during their question time session in each chamber. These questions can be either oral or written. Oral questions require an oral statement in the chamber, while a written question means the Member wants a written reply.
	Prime Minister's Questions (PMQs) – The Prime Minister answers questions from MPs every Wednesday from 12 pm until 12.30 pm when the House is sitting. The Leader of the Official Opposition, the second-largest party in Parliament, is allowed to ask six questions, again on any topic of their choice. The Leader of the SNP, as the next largest party in Parliament, is allowed to ask two questions. The rest of question time is then given over to backbench MPs to ask questions. MPs have to place their names on the order paper (the agenda for PMQs) and it is up to the Speaker who is called to ask a question. The PM clearly has to be well briefed on a range of topical issues in order to answer the questions. Some questions from their own party's MPs will have been suggested by the Whip's Office, so that they will have prepared responses. Most MPs are in the Chamber for this session, so it can become very noisy.
Work of committees	Much of the work of Parliament is done in committees of either House or joint committees of both Houses. There are committees established to consider draft laws. Select committees investigate the work of each government department and have a minimum of eleven members and now the majority of the chairs of these committees are elected; the number of chairs is allocated by party size in Parliament. These committees have full powers to call witnesses and demand answers to their questions. The government must respond to the reports of the Select committees within 60 days.
	There are also other select committees that assist with the working of Parliament and its business, such as the Backbench Business Committee that can select motions for certain debates, both in the Chamber and in Westminster Hall. This committee considers e-petitions that have gained more than 100,000 signatories on the government website and decides whether they should be debated.
Debates	Members of Parliament can also take part in parliamentary debates. Debates enable MPs and Lords to discuss government policy, propose new laws and current issues. At the end of a debate there can be a division when a vote has to be taken. The opposition parties are allocated days when they can propose motions for debate. The Speaker can also grant permission to hold emergency debates on topical issues.

Exam tip

If you get the chance, look at the Parliament channel on television and watch the work of Parliament live to see the content above in action. PMQs are also available on the BBC news website.

7 Where does political power reside?

The role of Members of Parliament (MPs)

REVISED

Members of Parliament (MPs) are elected to represent their constituency and all the people who live in the constituency. MPs divide their time between working in Parliament, in their constituency and working for their political party. Some MPs hold ministerial posts or shadow ministerial posts with specific responsibilities, which take up a lot of their time. Some MPs also have other jobs and outside interests. All of these now have to be registered and the details are published.

MPs' salaries

In 2017, the annual salary of an MP was £76,011 and they were also allowed to claim living expenses and office costs. In comparison, the Prime Minister's annual salary was £142,500. Government ministers also receive an additional salary on top of their MP's salary, as does the Leader of the Opposition and the Opposition Chief Whip.

Working in Parliament

When Parliament is in session, MPs spend a lot of their time working in the House of Commons. This work includes:
- dealing with constituency correspondence and issues
- raising issues affecting their constituents
- attending debates and voting on new laws
- attending functions relating both to their party politics and their political interests.

Most MPs are also members of select or standing committees, which look at issues of government policy or new laws.

Working in their constituency

Many MPs leave the House on Thursdays and return to their constituencies. They hold surgeries where they meet constituents and discuss their problems. There will also be a round of functions to attend from schools to local businesses as well as party-political functions in the constituency.

Helping their constituents

The local MP is there to assist all constituents with their problems. It is no good writing to another MP who might support your ideas to resolve a local issue because parliamentary convention states that a constituent has to work with their own MP. Many problems that MPs deal with are confidential and will not be made public. The MP may write to the government department or meet a minister on your behalf to resolve the issue. If it is an issue that can be made public, the MP can raise it in the House of Commons where it becomes a part of the official record and can come to the attention of the media. You may give your MP the authority to raise the issue outside Parliament, to seek publicity for the issue. MPs can also raise issues by:
- Questions – by asking ministers or the Prime Minister questions
- Adjournment debates – held for 30 minutes at the end of each day. Members can raise any issue in this debate
- Backbench debates – an MP can ask that the issue be raised in the time allocated for backbench debates. 35 days a year are set aside for these debates
- **Private Member's Bill** – an MP can put their name forward for the Private Member's Bill ballot that is held each year. If their name comes up near the top of the list and the issue they want to raise is uncontroversial, they stand a reasonable chance of introducing a bill that will become law.

> **Private Member's Bill** – a bill, a draft for a law, that is proposed by a MP. A lottery is held each year and if an MP comes out towards the top, they stand a chance of their bill becoming law.

> **Exam tip**
>
> Contact your local MP and ask them to visit your school or send them a questionnaire to complete. You can usually find out what they are doing on their websites.

Scrutiny role

MPs also have an important role to scrutinise proposed legislation, both on the floor of the House and in committee. This work is more fully outlined in the section about legislation (see page 60).

Ceremonial roles and key parliamentary roles

REVISED

There are a number of roles carried out that are necessary to the operation of our democratic process and the workings of Parliament as shown in Table 7.6.

Table 7.6 Key parliamentary roles

Parliamentary role	Commentary
The Speaker	The Speaker of the House of Commons is elected to the post by their fellow MPs. They chair debates in the Commons Chamber. The Speaker is the chief officer and has the highest authority in the Commons. The Speaker interprets the rules of the House. They can bar members, decide who speaks and can call ministers to the House to make statements.
	There are three Deputy Speakers who can also chair sittings of the House. They are also elected by their fellow MPs. They are known as:
	● the Chairman of Ways and Means
	● the First Deputy Chairman of Ways and Means
	● the Second Deputy Chairman of Ways and Means.
	Once elected, these MPs withdraw from any active political role.
	The **Lord Speaker** is elected by members of the House of Lords. Politically impartial, they are responsible for chairing the debates in the Lords chamber and offering advice on procedure.
Whips	Whips are MPs or Members of the House of Lords appointed by each party in Parliament to help organise parliamentary business and to ensure that their party's MPs turn out and vote according to the party's wishes.
	Every week, whips send out a notice (called 'The Whip') to their MPs and Lords detailing parliamentary business for the week and giving instructions on how to vote.
Frontbench MPs	Frontbenchers sit on the front green benches nearest to the Speaker in the House of Commons. On the government side this is where ministers sit, and on the opposition benches is where the shadow ministers representing the official opposition party sit.
Backbench MPs	A backbencher is an ordinary MP who holds no government or opposition post so therefore sits behind the front bench on the backbenches.
Black Rod	Black Rod is a senior officer in the House of Lords. They are responsible for its security. Black Rod is also the Secretary to the Lord Great Chamberlain and is responsible for and participates in the major ceremonial events at the Palace of Westminster, for example during the State Opening of Parliament.

The legislative process

Parliament deals with a range of different types of laws that are explained in the text box below.

Types of legislation

Bills (draft legislation) can be introduced by:
- the government
- individual MPs or Lords
- private individuals or organisations.

There are four different types of bill:
- **Public bills** – these change the law as it applies to the entire population and are the most common type of bill. They are proposed by government ministers.
- **Private bills** – these are usually promoted by organisations, like local authorities or private companies, to give them additional powers. They only change the law in regard to that one organisation or body.
- **Hybrid bills** – these mix the characteristics of public and private bills. The changes to the law proposed by a hybrid bill would affect the general public, but would also have a significant impact on specific individuals or groups. An example of a hybrid bill is the construction of the HS2 rail line.
- **Private members' bills** – a form of public bill as they affect the entire population, but they cannot involve raising taxation. They are introduced by MPs and Lords who are not government ministers. Often they are about social issues: for example, abortion, divorce or sexuality issues.

In order to become a law, an idea must be set out in writing. It then goes through various parliamentary stages before it is signed into law by the monarch. These stages are shown in Figure 7.3.

The Green Paper
Often the Government will publish a 'Green Paper', which is a discussion document about a possible new law, and invite MPs and others to comment upon its suggestions. It is called Green because the cover is green.

The First Reading
The Government then publishes a 'White Paper', which is a proposal for a new law. This becomes a Bill (draft law) and is formerly announced (First Reading) in the House of Commons. No debate takes place at this time.

The Second Reading
This stage involves a debate upon the principle of the proposed legislation and a vote takes place at the end of the debate.

The Committee Stage
This stage comes next, where a group of MPs from all parties discuss the Bill in detail, line by line, and vote on amendments.

The Report Stage
The work of the committee is discussed and voted upon in the House of Commons.

The Third Reading (or Final Stage)
The amended legislation is voted upon and the legislation is then sent to the House of Lords where all the same stages from First Reading to Third Reading are gone through. If the Lords make amendments, the Bill returns to the House of Commons where further votes take place until the Bill is accepted.

The Royal Assent
The legislation then receives Royal Assent – it is agreed and signed by the monarch – and then becomes Law.

Figure 7.3 How laws are made by Parliament

The formation of government

When a General Election is called all MPs stand down and, if they wish, become candidates for election. The Prime Minister and other ministers remain in post while no longer MPs so the work of government can continue. After the results are known the existing Prime Minister will go to Buckingham Palace and inform the monarch:
- that they have won the election, and the monarch will ask them to form a new government
- that they have lost, and that the monarch should ask the leader of the majority party to form a government
- that no party has won a majority.

Now test yourself and exam practice answers at **www.hoddereducation.co.uk/myrevisionnotes**

In theory the monarch can ask anyone to form a government but over time the convention described above has evolved. Since 2012 the timing of General Elections has been governed by the Fixed-term Parliament Act.

- In 2010 Prime Minister Gordon Brown did not win a majority of the seats and was unable to form a government so the Conservative leader David Cameron formed a coalition government with the Liberal Democrats, which gave the coalition a reasonable majority in the House of Commons.
- In 2015 the Conservatives won a majority of the seats so David Cameron continued as Prime Minister. He resigned in 2016 and was replaced by Theresa May; she called an election in 2017.
- In the 2017 General Election the Conservatives lost their majority but were still the largest party. Theresa May remained as Prime Minister and made a parliamentary deal with the DUP from Northern Ireland to ensure a parliamentary majority.

The role and powers of the Prime Minister, cabinet and ministers

REVISED

Prime Ministerial styles

- The phrase '*primus inter pares*' (first among equals), has been used to describe the role of the Prime Minister, but many recent Prime Ministers have been described as 'presidential' in the way they work.
- Many say Tony Blair, the Prime Minister from 1997 to 2008, operated a 'sofa-style government' where decisions were often made by small groups without civil servants present.
- The phrase 'first among equals' implies that the Prime Minister is one of a team – that is, the cabinet – and that the cabinet is of equal importance to the Prime Minister.
- The phrase 'cabinet government' is often used to describe how the British system operates. Where members of the cabinet agree important issues, they are then held by the concept of collective responsibility to support the policy even if they personally do not agree with it. The role of a Prime Minister at a cabinet meeting is to sum up the views of its members and state what he or she thinks the 'agreed' position is. If ministers speak out in public against the cabinet decision, they must resign.

Prime Minister's Office

- Prime Ministers are supported by their own office support structure which itself mirrors all the work of government.
- Although much of this work is co-ordinated through the Cabinet Office, the Prime Minister will also have a private office staff that organises his or her schedule, but also provides a link to the party in Parliament and the country.
- A large media team also supports the Prime Minister.
- After the 2017 General Election Prime Minister Theresa May had to sack her two closest aides as ministers and others felt they held too much power and were responsible for the poor performance of the Conservative party election campaign.

Role of the Prime Minister

The Prime Minister has a number of roles:

- leader of their political party and responsible for its operation
- head of government, responsible for appointing the cabinet and junior ministers
- increasingly seen as the spokesperson for the UK aboard and at international events and summits
- provides the political direction of the government
- responsible and accountable to Parliament for the action of the government
- often the spokesperson for the nation at times of crisis events
- a constituency MP carrying out the normal duties of an MP
- holds weekly meeting with the monarch.

The Prime Minister also chairs cabinet meetings; there are also a number of cabinet committees that the Prime Minister agrees to set up and the Prime Minister appoints the chairs of these committees. The committees report to the cabinet.

Cabinet and ministers

- The Prime Minister appoints their own cabinet.
- The current cabinet consists of 21 other members, and there are then a further 97 junior ministers.
- The size of the cabinet is not limited, but the number that can have a ministerial salary is.
- The senior posts within the cabinet have traditionally been: the Chancellor of the Exchequer, the Foreign Secretary, the Home Secretary and the Defence Secretary.
- All ministers can be sacked by the Prime Minister at any time.
- Each government department has a senior minister and a number of junior ministers who cover areas of the department's work and members of the House of Lords who answer departmental questions in the Lords.

The organisation of government administration and the role of the civil service

REVISED

Ministers attend cabinet meetings and also each run a government department supported by a number of junior ministers. A full list of cabinet members can be found at https://www.gov.uk/government/ministers. Government ministers who are accountable to Parliament run the government. There are also 361 agencies and other public bodies and 72 high-profile groups, eleven public corporations, and the 3 devolved administrations that also work with the departments. The structure can vary from government to government. Departments can be renamed, merged or disappear. For more details of government structure visit https://www.gov.uk/government/organisations.

Agencies are business units at arm's length from government that carry out specific functions or services on behalf of their client government department. The term used to cover the range of differing agency arrangements is **non-departmental public bodies (NDPBs)**. They are also known by the term **quango** (quasi autonomous non-government organisations). Since 2010, the government policy has been to cut down on the number of government-linked quangos.

NDPBs – non-departmental public bodies, formerly quangos.

Quangos – quasi autonomous non-government organisations. These are bodies that work with government, sometimes carrying out services on behalf of government and funded by government, but partially independent from government. Government now uses the term NDPBs to describe them, as the term quango is associated with negative media coverage of these bodies.

The role of the civil service

The civil service helps the government develop and implement its policy. It also provides services directly to the public, including running prisons, employment services, the benefits and pension system and issuing driving licences. In recent years, the number of civil servants has declined as more government services are provided on an agency basis; their employees are then not directly employed civil servants. In March 2016 there were 386,620 full-time equivalent (FTE) civil service employees. This amounts to 35 per cent of civil service staff levels in 1945 and less than half the employees in 1976 (751,000).

Civil servants are politically neutral, are impartial and remain in post when governments change. They are also anonymous to the public, but increasingly those in NDPBs are becoming accountable and are often called before parliamentary committees. The Senior Civil Service (SCS) is made up of the top 3600 civil servants who devise policy and advise ministers. Civil servants in this group earn between £60,000 and £140,000.

Exam tip

It is not necessary to remember the names of actual government ministers; just be able to recall some of the range of posts within government, especially the top four.

Websites

- UK government: www.gov.uk
- BBC News: www.bbc.co.uk/news/election/2017/results
- UK Parliament: www.parliament.uk
- House of Lords: www.parliament.uk/lords
- Electoral Reform Society: www.electoral-reform.org.uk
- Courts and Tribunals Judiciary: www.judiciary.gov.uk
- Supreme Court: www.supremecourt.uk
- British Monarchy: www.royal.gov.uk
- Prime Minister's Office: www.gov.uk/government/organisations/prime-ministers-office-10-downing-street
- Parliamentary publications:
  www.publications.parliament.uk/pa/cm/cmregmem.htm
  www.parliament.uk/about/mps-and-lords/members/pay-mps/

Now test yourself

TESTED

1 Explain the role of the Speaker in the House of Commons.
2 Define what is meant by the expression a 'coalition government'.
3 Name a voting system used in the UK.
4 Identify a general election where no party won an overall majority.

Answers online

Exam practice

1 Using Table 7.1 on page 50 showing the number of MPs elected and each party's percentage of the national vote, describe the options for forming the new government if the election had been based upon a proportional voting system. [4]
2 Analyse the main policy differences between the major parties at the 2017 General Election. [8]
3*If you were an active citizen wishing to bring about a change in government policy examine whether you would be more likely to succeed if you were a member of a pressure group or a backbench MP? In your answer you should consider:
   - the ways in which pressure groups operate
   - the opportunities for backbench MPs to bring about change. [8]

ONLINE

8 How do others govern themselves?

Electoral systems and processes used in European parliamentary elections and their impact on political parties

When elections to the European Parliament (the Parliament of the European Union) were first held in the UK, MEPs (Members of the European Parliament) were elected using the first past the post (FPTP) electoral system in England, Scotland and Wales. The country was split into single member constituencies and each elector had one vote. The candidate with most votes was elected.

In Northern Ireland, the single transferrable vote (STV) system was used to ensure that by using a proportional system the minority Nationalist community would gain one of the three seats. The whole of Northern Ireland is one constituency and voters place the candidates in order of their preference. A quota system is used to count the votes.

The European Parliamentary Elections Act of 1999 changed the voting system from FPTP to a closed party list system. Now, the country is split into twelve regions, with varying numbers of MEPs according to the population for each region. The closed list system allowed voters to use the single 'X' system against a name of a party. The party has a list of candidates it has placed in number order. The number of votes achieved by the party is then converted into MEPs elected. If a party wins two seats, candidate numbers 1 and 2 from its list are elected. The voter has no say in this system about whom they elect, only the party they support. It is the party that decides which candidates are top or bottom of their list.

Elections for the European Parliament are held every five years. The next elections are due in 2019, and this is one of the reasons given for the triggering of Article 50 regarding the UK leaving the EU by March 2019. The EU insists that member countries use a proportional system of voting for members of the European Parliament hence the change made in the UK in 1999. This system ensures that a range of views are represented in the Parliament. The charts below show the UK representations in the European Parliament after the last elections in 2014.

Table 8.1 The turnout for European Parliamentary elections

Election year	% turnout
1979	32.34
1984	32.57
1989	36.37
1994	36.43
1999	24.0
2004	38.52
2009	34.7
2014	35.6

One of the issues regarding European elections in the UK has been voter turnout. It is about equal to that for local council elections in the UK.

Voters in the European elections often vote on national issues and against their own government of the time rather than on transnational European issues. The UK political parties that contest these elections belong to transnational party political groups in the European Parliament.

In the European Parliament, MEPs sit in **transnational groups** made up of at least fifteen MEPs as members from seven member countries. The Parliament sits in a horseshoe design by party group (see Figure 8.1), like many continental parliaments. Remember the European Parliament is not as powerful as most national parliaments.

- The UK Conservative MEPs sit in the ECR group.
- Labour MEPs sit in the S&D group.
- The Greens sit in the Green/EFA group.
- UKIP MEPs sit in the EFD group.
- Lib Dem MEPs sit in the ALDE group.

> **Transnational groupings** – a political grouping in the European Parliament made up of MEPs from several countries.

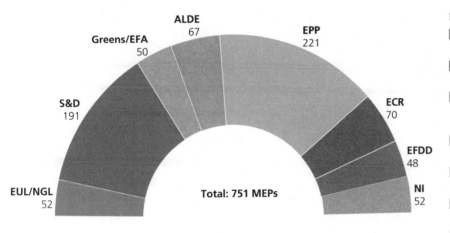

Key

- ██ EUL/NGL – European United Left-Nordic Green Left (left-wing)
- ██ S&D – Progressive Alliance of Socialists and Democrats in Europe (centre-left)
- ██ Greens/EFA – Greens/European Free Alliance (Greens and regionalists/nationalists)
- ██ ALDE – Alliance of Liberals and Democrats for Europe (liberal)
- ██ EPP – European People's Party (Christian Democrats)
- ██ ECR – European Conservatives and Reformists Group (right-wing)
- ██ EFD – Europe of Freedom and Democracy (Eurosceptic)
- ██ NA – Non-attached (MEPs not part of any group)

Figure 8.1 Groups in European Parliament

Citizen participation in politics in one democratic and one non-democratic political system outside the UK

REVISED

Many countries use the word democratic in their title or describe themselves as democratic but do not meet up to the demands set out in earlier chapters about what makes a democratic society. To assist your revision, copy Table 8.2 and choose a country you think is **non-democratic** then check it against the criteria identified in the table regarding what makes a democracy.

> **Non-democratic** – a system of government that lacks some or all of the elements that make up a democratic political system.

Table 8.2 Democracy checklist

Democracy criteria	Non-democratic country's position
There are parties or groups competing for power.	
There are time limits on persons holding office before fresh elections.	
There are regular elections.	
All groups in society should be able to vote without any unfair barriers.	
The elections are open and fair.	
The voting system is not biased.	
Power is easily transferred from one government to another.	
There is a free press and media and no censorship.	
People have freedom of expression.	
People have freedom to worship.	
People have freedom of assembly.	
People are free to join political parties or pressure groups.	
Trade unions and other groups are free to operate.	
There is no detention without trial.	
The judiciary is free and independent.	
Corruption is not practised in public life.	
The police force is not a political tool to be used by any one group and is free from corruption.	
The military are not active in politics and are subject to legal controls.	

So, what do we mean by a non-democratic system? Table 8.3 sets out different types of non-democratic political systems.

Table 8.3 Different types of non-democratic political systems

Non-democratic form of government	Comment
Absolute monarchy	A traditional form of government in which power is held by one family based upon a hereditary principle of power being transferred down a royal line. A small number of countries still have an absolute monarchy. Most monarchies are now are called constitutional monarchies, where the monarch has passed all or most of their powers to an elected government and the monarch is a symbol of national unity. The UK is an example of a constitutional monarchy. Examples of absolute monarchies are: Brunei, Oman, Qatar, Saudi Arabia, Swaziland.
Dictatorship	A system of government where there is rule by one person or group. Examples would be the Presidents of Syria, Mauritania and Gabon. Freedom House identified 49 dictatorships in its 2015 Annual Report. Many of these also happen to be absolute monarchs or heads of single-party states.
Authoritarian rule	This is where power is in the hands of a leader or a small group that is not constitutionally accountable to the people. Authoritarian leaders rule outside the existing laws and legal framework. Citizens do not have normally a chance to free themselves of their rule by the electoral process. This form of rule is often seen when the military takes over a state. For example, the current government in Egypt was formed following a military takeover. However, although a president was elected after the takeover, because he was the ex-military chief and because of the circumstances of the election and the situation in Egypt, there is a system of authoritarian rule in place.

→

Non-democratic form of government	Comment
Military	Where the government is run by the military, the phrase 'military junta' is often used to describe the group of military officers running a country. Examples of military juntas are Thailand and Myanmar.
One-party state	This describes a system that only allows one political party to hold power. There may be elections, but the candidates will belong to the one party and there may be no choice of candidates on the ballot paper. Examples of one-party states are China, Cuba, Eritrea, Laos, Vietnam and the Western Sahara.
Oligarchy	This is a system whereby the state and economy are controlled by a small group of well-placed, extremely wealthy insiders. These people could be formed from royalty, the wealthy, due to family ties, education, corporate power, or from the military. This system can sit alongside differing forms of democracy. It is often used to describe how the Russian system of government works alongside the elected government members.
Aristocracy	This is government by the few usually based upon inherited wealth and status in society. In the UK for many centuries this power of the nobility/aristocracy worked alongside the power of the monarch.
Theocracy	This is where the government of the state is held by religious figures whose beliefs dominate the governmental system. Examples are Iran and the Vatican.
Technocracy	A government system based upon people who are not elected but are technical experts in their field. Sometimes in a crisis other forms of governments resort to technocrats in order to resolve a crisis situation. An example would be the appointment of the government in Greece in 2011, to deal with its economic crisis.

Websites

- Freedom House: www.freedomhouse.org
- Global Witness: www.globalwitness.org/en
- Amnesty International UK: www.amnesty.org.uk
- European Parliament: www.europarl.europa.eu/portal/en

Now test yourself

TESTED

1 Define using an example what is meant by an 'absolute monarchy'.
2 Explain what is meant by the phrase 'a transnational political group' in the context of the European Parliament.
3 Identify one important characteristic of a democracy.
4 Name a country that can be described as having a military dictatorship.

Answers online

Exam practice

1 Study Figure 8.1 on page 65 which shows the composition of the European Parliament. Describe in what ways the layout and composition of the European Parliament differ from the current UK Parliament. [4]
2 Justify the claim that the United Kingdom is a fully-functioning democracy. [8]
3* To what extent is it important that in a democracy the rights of the media and the press are safeguarded?
In your answer you should consider:
- the role of the media in society
- the relationship a political system and the media. [8]

ONLINE

9 What are the principles and values of British society?

The key principles and values underpinning British society today

REVISED

Politicians are often quoted in the media using the expression '**British values**'. This phrase means those values associated with contemporary British society. The issue of British values came onto the political agenda in the early 2000s, following the increase in terrorist threat to the UK, the debate about the increase in migration to the UK and the success of **multiculturalism** as a policy. It does not mean that these values are solely British or that the British invented them.

Most values in any society are based upon the culture, religious nature and history of that society. Many values and **principles** are now seen as universal and are identified in international law or treaties such as the **Universal Declaration of Human Rights** or the **Human Rights Act** 1998 in the United Kingdom.

In June 2014, the government announced that schools would be required to promote British values from September of that year. The move followed concerns about a perceived promotion of strict Islamist values in some schools in Birmingham.

According to the Department for Education (DfE) the fundamental British values are:
- democracy
- the **rule of law**
- individual liberty
- mutual respect for and tolerance of those with different faiths and beliefs and for those without faith.

What can be debated and discussed as citizenship topics are how these terms are defined and what do they mean in practice.
- What makes a country truly democratic?
- Does the rule of law guarantee equal treatment by the law?
- When does individual liberty infringe on the rights of others?
- How much tolerance can a society show to those who do not share its values?

British values – the values that are associated with living in modern-day Britain.

Multiculturalism/ multicultural society – a society that consists of people from a range of cultural and religious backgrounds.

Principle – a basic truth or idea that underpins a system of beliefs associated with a given society.

Universal Declaration of Human Rights – an international law setting out a set of universal human rights under the auspices of the United Nations.

Human Rights Act (HRA) – this was passed in 1998 and came into force in 2000. This Act brought together numerous pieces of human rights legislation and gave UK citizens easier access to the European Court of Human Rights.

The rule of law – a basic principle of a democratic society that the law applies equally to all people.

The human, moral, legal and political rights and the duties, equalities and freedoms of citizens

REVISED

While we use the words and phrases 'rights', 'responsibilities', 'freedoms' and 'the rule of law' in everyday conversation, in regard to citizenship they have exact meanings. There is also the debate within society about the balance between rights and responsibilities/duties. What rights should citizens have and what duties or responsibilities can the state expect from its citizens? For example, in a time of war the state increases the duties it places upon its citizens – from calling up to fight to rationing food – and limits citizens' rights, for example freedom of movement and speech.

Now test yourself and exam practice answers at **www.hoddereducation.co.uk/myrevisionnotes**

- **Rights** are the legal binding, social and ethical entitlements that are considered the building blocks of a society. All citizens within our society enjoy them equally. The idea of freedom of speech is an essential part of our way of life, but society does limit that right where your right conflicts with other rights. Rights within a society structure the way government operates, the content of laws and the morality of society. Rights are often grouped together and debates take place about human rights or children's rights or prisoner's rights, for example.
- **Morals** are the rules that govern which actions are believed to be right and which are wrong. They are often related to personal behaviour. A society can claim to live by certain moral values and individuals can state that they live their life by certain moral values.
- **Duties/responsibilities** (these two terms often are interchangeable, but the term duty often implies a legal/moral underpinning) relate to those responsibilities placed upon its citizens by a society. For example, you are expected to pay your taxes, obey the law and take part in the judicial system as a jury member if required. Duties are not optional and are often enshrined in law.
- **Freedoms** are the power or right to speak and act or think as one wants. We often explain freedom in relation to a context. Expressions such as freedom of choice, the freedom of the press and freedom of movement relate to some basic beliefs in our society.
- **Equality** means treating all individuals equally. Where inequality or discrimination occur, the state often attempts to remedy the situation either through policy or legislative action.

> **Exam tip**
>
> It is helpful to answer any questions about such terms by using an example to indicate your ability both to understand the question and apply your knowledge.

Table 9.1 Examples of legislative changes to individual rights and equality issues in the UK

Rights of women	Sexual rights
Representation of the People Act 1928	The Sexual Offences Act 1967
Equal Pay Act 1970	Civil Partnerships Act 2005
Equality Acts 2006 and 2010	Sexual Offences Act 2003
Sex Discrimination Acts 1975 and 1986	The Gender Recognition Act 2004
Employment and Equality Regulations 2003 and 2006	Marriage (Same Sex Couples) Act 2013
	Disability Discrimination Act 1995 and 2005
	The Special Needs and Disability Act 2001
Racial equality	**Rights of the child**
Race Relations Acts 1965, 1968, 1976 and 2000	The United Nations Convention on the Rights of the Child came into force in 1992–every child in the UK is entitled to over 40 specific rights

Race audit could lead to new laws

The UK government in 2017 published consolidated data for the first time that indicated the experience of public services by differing racial groups in the UK. The government stated that the information contained in the data may lead to changes in legislation to attempt to overcome some of the issued raised. To find out more about what this data tells us about the UK today use the following web site: https://www.ethnicity-facts-figures.service.gov.uk

Key factors that create individual, group, national and global identities

The factors that create **identity** are multi-dimensional and they influence different individuals in different ways. Table 9.2 identifies some factors that influence the creation of identity.

Identity – the characteristics that determine who or what a person is.

Group identity – the identity associated with belonging to a group.

National identity – an identity associated with being a citizen of a specific country.

Global identity – the concept that some aspects of identity are now global in nature.

Table 9.2 Factors that influence the creation of identity

Identity	Factors		Comment
Individual	● Gender ● Education ● Race ● Employment ● Family ● Peer group	● Ethnic group ● Location ● Social class ● Culture ● Religion ● Media	Each of these factors can have varying level of importance for each individual.
Group	● Employment ● Peer group ● Social interests ● Political views		While these repeat individual identity factors they also represent groups to which one is attached and can therefore allow one to be influenced by the identity of the group.
National	● Shared values ● Homogeneity		National identity and its association with national values gets confused with national characteristics and stereotyping. Factors influencing national identity could be the role of monarchy providing a feeling of continuity.
Global	● Political and social awareness		Increasingly in this inter-connected world of 24-hour news, individuals can readily identify with global issues and concerns.

For each individual, group or nation identity and the weight given to any, all or more than those factors listed can vary from person to person, group to group and from one nation to another.

National identity can also relate to the nature of the society within which one lives and works. In the UK we have a British identity, others have a Scottish, Welsh, English, Irish or Cornish identity that they would put before or in place of their British identity. National identity can also link back to shared values, as long as citizens believe and support those values that the nation-state holds together.

Websites

Office for National Statistics: www.ons.gov.uk – A UK government site that publishes statistics and background papers about the nature of the UK

The process of becoming a UK citizen: www.gov.uk/becoming-a-british-citizen – This website allows you to consider what we mean by citizenship and national identity through the spectrum of someone who wishes to become a British citizen

http://esol.britishcouncil.org/content/learners/uk-life/life-uk-test/values-and-principles-uk – This is a guide about British values for those living overseas

Now test yourself

1 Identify one key British value.
2 Define what is meant by a citizen's duties.
3 Name one factor that influences an individual's identity.
4 Explain using an example how government has tried to overcome an inequality in society.

Answers online

Exam practice

IF THE UK FLAG WAS DIVIDED LIKE UK WEALTH

1% WOULD OWN THIS

9% WOULD OWN THIS

THE REMAINING 90% WOULD OWN THIS

Source: hmrc.gov.uk/stats/personal_wealth/13-5-table-2005.pdf

WE'RE NOT ALL IN THIS TOGETHER

1 How do you consider belonging to each of the three groups indicated in the picture above would impact upon a person's identity? [4]
2 Make a case to justify the selection of the four fundamental British values identified by the British government. [8]
3* Evaluate the case that states that the media is an important factor in influencing individual identity. In your answer you should consider:
  ● the range of factors than can influence individual identity
  ● differing formats of the media and their influence. [8]

ONLINE

10 What do we mean by identity?

The key question for this section is 'What do we mean and understand by identity?' There are many ways in which one can study aspects of identity from individual to group to societal. All three aspects will be considered within this chapter.

The United Kingdom of Great Britain and Northern Ireland and identity debates

This element of the course looks at the composition of the current United Kingdom and the relationship of the components with regard to identity. In this context it is about regional, national and British identity.

In order to understand the nature of national and other identities it is important to understand the relationship of the populations within each of the nations of the UK, which clearly show the dominance of the population of England.

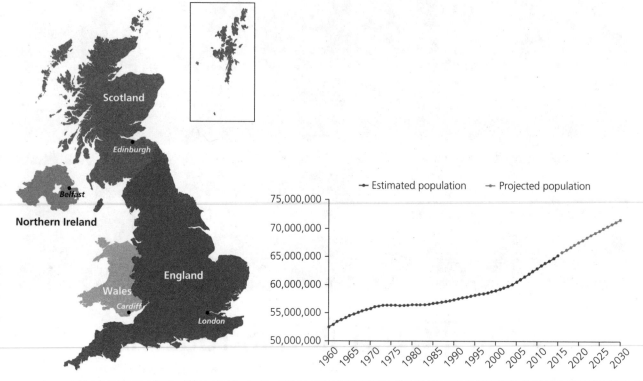

Figure 10.1 The nations of the UK

Figure 10.2 Projected growth in the UK population to 2030

Table 10.1 The UK population, 2016

Country	Population (2016)	% of total
United Kingdom	65,110,000	100.00
England	54,786,300	84.14
Scotland	5,373,000	8.25
Wales	3,099,100	4.76
Northern Ireland	1,851,600	2.84

...our UK countries over
...n.

...700 (up 0.86 per cent) to
...he UK's population.

...400 (up 0.47 per cent) to
...e UK's population.

... (up 0.23 per cent) to
...e UK's population.

...ased by 11,100 (up 0.60 per
...cent of the UK's population.

...future trends it is also important
...lation. A nation with an ageing
...h a rising number of young people.

...ulation, 1974 to 2039 (projected)

% population aged 16 to 64	% population aged 65 and over
61.0	13.8
64.1	14.9
63.4	15.8
64.5	15.9
63.5	17.7
61.1	19.9
58.5	23.3
57.9	24.3

Table 10.2 clearly indicates how it is projected that the percentage of young people in the UK is declining, the percentage of population of traditional working age is also declining while there is and will continue to be a steady increase in the percentage of over-65s in the UK.

All these factors are and will influence decision-makers, politicians and voters for years to come.

The impact of this on identity debates

The UK operated as a centralised state with all political power centred on London and Parliament, until the start of devolution. Identity within the nations and regions of the United Kingdom has related to historical situations, for example Scotland has different education and legal systems than do the rest of the UK. National identity within these nations has been shown through cultural identity, based upon literature, customs, music, language and sport.

● Northern Ireland, which only came into existence in 1921 as a result of the establishment of the then Irish free State (now the Irish Republic), has a divided cultural identity between those who are nationalist and support the re-unification of Ireland and the unionists who support Northern Ireland and its union with the UK. Within Northern Ireland the identity factors based upon culture follow the two strands within society: each identifies with differing sports, one supports a recognition of the Irish language the other does not.

Exam tip

While the topic involves an understanding of figures what is important is not remembering statistics but being able to write about trends, and being able to draw together differing figures to outline a case or make an argument. So don't get lost in numbers, just remember what picture the numbers paint.

- In Wales the national identity is shown through the cultural factors indicated above, from the importance of Welsh rugby to the Eisteddfod.
- Within England regions and counties have traditions and cultural identities where they seek to indicate a clear identity. Areas like the West Country, especially Cornwall, and counties like Yorkshire and Lancashire promote their own identities.

With the increasing movement of people within the United Kingdom and increasing migration to the UK, some of these identity factors may not be so important across the entire population.

The impact of this national debate about identity can be seen as one of the factors that have led to the growth in the devolution of power to the nations and regions of the UK. Scotland once again has its own Parliament, Wales and Northern Ireland their own Assemblies, so more decisions that impact upon the lives of the people of those nations are decided by their own politicians in their own capital cities. Will the recognition of separate identities within the United Kingdom lead to the breakup of the United Kingdom? Already Scotland has had a referendum on independence.

Is there a clear acceptance by the population of what it means to be British? Do the British have a clear identity, or is it a matter of being Scottish, Welsh, Irish or English first and British second? All the values and principles that underpin society are shared values and are also shared by numerous other countries. The importance of being British is often summed up by the political slogan 'Stronger together', which was used to persuade people in Scotland to continue to support the Union.

Changes and movement of population over time: the impact on communities; immigration and migration to and from the UK

REVISED

Like many other countries the United Kingdom has been invaded and conquered, has conquered other countries and has accepted people from across the world to settle and live permanently in the individual countries. Figure 10.3 shows how our society has evolved over the centuries.

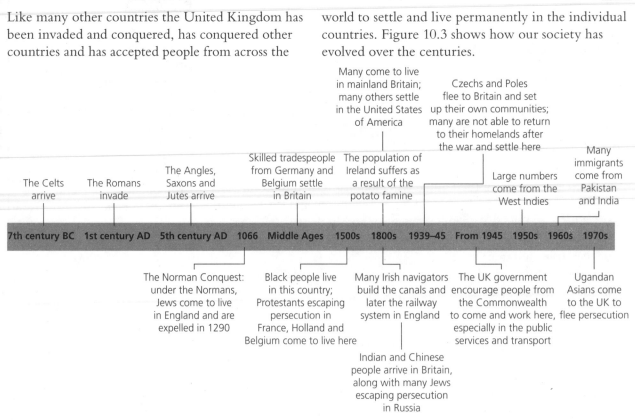

Figure 10.3 How UK society has evolved

Migration and the EU

Since 1973 the UK has been a member of the European Union. The concept of free movement of labour throughout the EU has meant that many EU citizens have come to the UK to live and work. Nearly 1.2 million UK citizens live and work in the EU. Just over 1 million of these live in Spain. Of this 1.2 million, around 400,000 are claiming a UK state pension. It is estimated that 3.3 million EU citizens live in the UK; of these 2.1 million are in work and the remaining 1.2 million are dependents.

The impact on different communities in the UK

The impacts of a changing population have varied from community to community. In the 19th century there was a large-scale movement of population within the UK from the countryside to towns and a growth of many towns into today's large cities. For example, Manchester saw its population grow by 600 per cent between 1771 and 1831. Bradford's population grew by 50 per cent every ten years between 1811 and 1851. In 1851, only 50 per cent of its population had been born in Bradford. In the 20th century many towns and cities have seen changing patterns of population movement.

> **Exam tip**
>
> Look at the population data for your own local community and compare this with the numbers 100 years ago. This can be done by an internet search. Use figures from the Office of National Statistics and your local council data.

Case studies of the impact of population changes

Table 10.3 indicates some of the arguments made in favour of and against immigration.

Table 10.3 Arguments for and against immigration

Arguments in favour of immigration	Issues arising from immigration
Cheap labour	Language problems
Helps overcome labour shortages	Racial/ethnic tensions
Immigrants are often prepared to do unskilled jobs	Jobs lost to incoming workers
Some immigrants are highly skilled	By employing high skilled migrant labour the government avoids the costs involved in developing the UK skills base
Cultural diversity	Pressure on housing and local services especially where large numbers of migrants settle to work
	Limited skills/education in immigrant population

The information shown on Table 10.3 was based upon research undertaken in 4 areas of the UK each with a different experience of immigration. Where there was a long tradition of migration and a high ethic population diversity had become a normal part of everyday life. The picture was different where the population changes had been more recent. One of the areas studied had seen the share of immigrants increase 500% in 10 years for 2001 to 2011. This resulted in a sense amongst some of the population of bitterness and others expressed concerns about the pressure on public services.

The nature of migration in the UK

Figure 10.4 shows long-term international net migration in the UK by nationality.

Exam tip

Remember that the net migration figure is the difference between those leaving and those arriving in the UK.

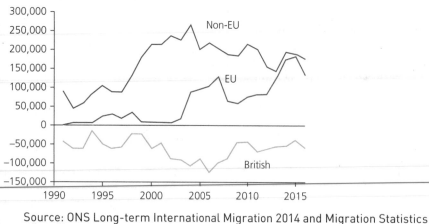

Source: ONS Long-term International Migration 2014 and Migration Statistics Quarterly Report, May 2017

Figure 10.4 Migration by nationality

Key fact

One of the major discussions regarding immigration figures is that they include students who come to the UK to attend colleges and universities then return to their home countries. Many argue that students should be excluded from the migration totals.

Figure 10.5 shows reasons people have given for migrating to the UK.

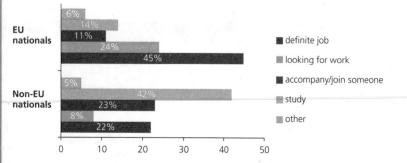

Source: ONS Migration Statistics Quarterly Report, May 2017

Figure 10.5 Reasons for migrating to the UK

Mutual respect and understanding in a diverse society; the values that underpin democratic society

REVISED

In 2011, the then Conservative Prime Minister David Cameron made a speech claiming that multiculturalism had failed. He defined state multiculturalism as a policy that 'encouraged different cultures to live separate lives, apart from each other and apart from the mainstream'. He claimed that the UK needed a clear sense of shared national identity that is open to everyone. He then outlined the values he associated with this sense of national identity as:

- freedom of speech
- freedom of worship
- democracy
- the rule of law
- equal rights regardless of race, sex or sexuality.

Now test yourself and exam practice answers at **www.hoddereducation.co.uk/myrevisionnotes**

He also said 'We must say to our citizens: this is what defines us as a society. To belong here is to believe in these things.' These are shared values associated with all modern Western liberal democracies and are included in human rights agreements.

It is important to remember that all of these values and freedoms have limits:

Freedom of speech: Can you have total freedom of speech? Can you say anything about anybody or anything? No – there are legal limits.

Freedom of worship: There is freedom to worship or not to worship. Society does not impose a set of religious beliefs upon its citizens.

Democracy: The UK claims to be a democracy. Citizens are entitled to vote and can elect representatives or stand for election themselves.

The rule of law: All citizens are equal before the law and have equal access and will be treated the same according to the offence committed not according to their background.

Equal rights: All citizens have their rights protected and should not be subject to discrimination.

In order to bring about the changes he wanted, David Cameron believed there were a number of practical things that could be done:

- Immigrants should speak English.
- Britishness classes and British history should be taught in schools.
- The National Citizenship Service was introduced for 16-year-olds.
- Developing the nature of the concept of the Big Society – relating to voluntary activity by citizens.

The concept of multiculturalism has underpinned the nature of UK society since 1945. Multiculturalism refers to the idea of differing peoples and groups living alongside each other in harmony and having respect for their cultural and religious differences. Three possible options have been suggested for the future path of multiculturalism:

1 **Ethnic groups** integrate into wider society. They begin to influence the **dominant culture** of the country, the **culture** evolves over time and **cultural integration** occurs.

2 The **ethnic groups integrate** into society, they retain their own **culture**, while adopting all, or some aspects of, the **dominant culture** of the country; people have **multiple identities**. The **ethnic groups** live alongside the **indigenous** population.

3 **Ethnic groups** do not integrate into wider society; they retain their own **culture** and reject the **dominant culture**.

> **Multiple identity** – a person can assume different identities at different times and in different situations.

Identity and multiple identities; the diverse nature of the UK population

REVISED

Individuals gain their identity in numerous ways. Some people study the impact of a person's biological background, while others study the nature of how people are brought up. This scientific discussion is called the **nature versus nurture** debate. It revolves around which of these two aspects is most important in an individual's personal development and the creation of their identity.

> **Nature versus nurture** – a debate about whether a person's personality and identity are most affected by their biological background or by the way in which they are brought up.

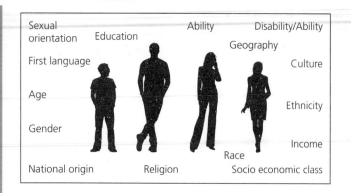

Figure 10.6 Factors that create identity

In essence identity is about a sense of belonging or attachment.

- As Figure 10.6 shows individual identity relates to one's relationship with a range of characteristics.
- Group identity relates to 'groups' in the broader sense that one is associated. That can be the peer group (those people of your own age that you associated with), formal or informal groups and supporting a sporting team to belonging to a voluntary group or organisation.
- Multiple identities relates to the fact that at different times and in different situations a person may adopt an identity based upon a range of different aspects of identity. For example, the Manchester United supporter who comes from a Pakistani background and supports Pakistan against England when watching a test cricket match.

The diverse nature of the UK population

Figure 10.7 indicates the changing pattern of the UK population from 2001 to 2011. The figures relate to the percentage change over the period.

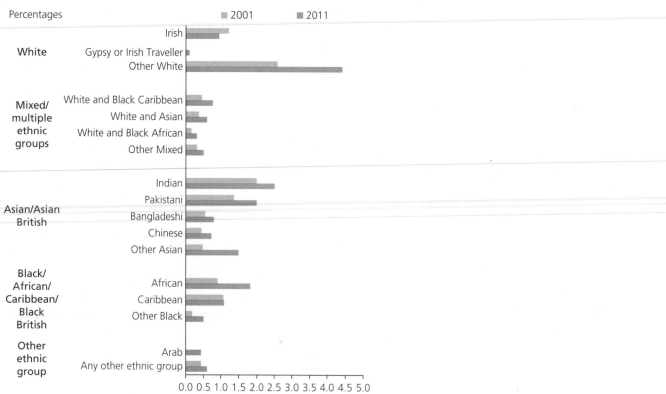

Figure 10.7 The changing pattern of the UK population from 2001 to 2011

This graph indicates that it is difficult to draw national conclusions; rather one must study regional patterns from which to draw evidence (see Table 10.4).

Table 10.4 Local authorities with the highest and lowest proportion of White British, Any Other White and Indian ethnic groups

White British (80.5% of UK population		Any other White (4.4% of the UK population)		Indian (2.5% of the UK population)	
Highest %					
Redcar	97.6	Kensington and Chelsea	28.9	Leicester	28.3
Allerdale	97.6	Westminster	24.1	Harrow	26.4
Staffordshire	97.5	Haringey	23.0	Hounslow	19.0
Blaenau Gwent	97.3	Hammersmith and Fulham	19.6	Brent	18.6
Copeland	97.3	Camden	19.0	Oadby and Wigston	17.7
Lowest %					
Newham	16.7	Redcar	0.6	Isles of Scilly	0.0
Brent	18.0	Torfaen	0.6	Torridge	0.1
Ealing	30.4	Knowsley	0.7	Rydaye	0.1
Harrow	30.9	South Tyneside	0.7	Redcar	0.1
Tower Hamlets	31.2	South Staffordshire	0.7	Purbeck	0.1

The UK population is made up of citizens from a variety of countries

In 2015, Poland was the most common non-UK country of birth for citizens of the UK. Between 2004 and 2014, India had been the most common. An estimated 831,000 residents of the UK were born in Poland (9.7 per cent of the total number of non-UK-born residents in the UK in 2015). This is more than eight times higher than in 2004, when 94,000 residents of the UK were born in Poland. Between 2004 and 2015 there has been a statistically significant increase of 737,000 residents in the UK who were born in Poland.

In 2015, the five most common countries of birth for residents born outside the UK were:

1 Poland (831,000)
2 India (795,000)
3 Pakistan (503,000)
4 Republic of Ireland (382,000)
5 Germany (286,000)

National identity

When asked about British identity a survey found that the following characteristics were seen to be important if one wished to be described as British (survey results in brackets):

- to have British **citizenship** (85 per cent)
- to have been born in Britain (74 per cent)
- to have lived here for most of your life (77 per cent)
- to respect political institutions and laws (85 per cent)
- to be able to speak English (95 per cent)
- to be a Christian (24 per cent)
- to feel British (78 per cent)
- to have British ancestry (51 per cent)
- to share customs/traditions (50 per cent).

Another survey has found that:

- There was some shift in the late twentieth century away from a British identity towards separate Scottish or English (and perhaps Welsh) identities.
- The great majority of the population continues to subscribe to one of the four national identities of Great Britain and most have 'dual' (multiple) identities.

Unlike in some other countries national identity within the UK is made more complex by the UK itself being a merger of four national identities. Remember that national identity can incorporate values and attitudes, but increasingly the values and principles underpinning life in the UK are universal values.

> **Citizenship** – a legal status conferred by a state upon members of the state, indicating their membership of the state.

Websites

- British Social Attitudes Survey: www.bsa-data.natcen.ac.uk – Regularly reviews survey evidence about social issues within the UK
- Migration Watch: www.migrationwatchuk.org/statistics-net-migration-statistics – A think tank that investigates migration issues
- Office of National Statistics: https://www.ons.gov.uk/peoplepopulationandcommunity/populationandmigration – Official government body for statistical information
- UK Parliament: researchbriefings.files.parliament.uk/documents/SN06077/SN06077.pdf – Research paper regarding EU migration to the UK 2017

Now test yourself

TESTED

1 Identify one of the nations of the UK.
2 Define what is meant by 'multiple identity'.
3 Name the country that had the largest number of its citizens migrate to the UK in 2015.
4 Explain what is meant by the phrase 'net migration'.

Answers online

Exam practice

1 Use Table 10.4 on page 79 to discuss how issues relating to multiculturalism can differ in different parts of the UK. [4]
2 Justify the argument made by David Cameron in 2012 that multiculturalism in the UK has failed. [8]
3*Analyse the evidence that the growth of separate national identities in the United Kingdom will lead to the breakup of the United Kingdom as a state.
   In your answer you should consider:
   - the nature of national identities within the UK
   - political developments that might lead to the breakup of the UK. [8]

ONLINE

Now test yourself and exam practice answers at **www.hoddereducation.co.uk/myrevisionnotes**

11 What is the role of the media and the free press?

The rights, responsibilities and role of the media

The media has rights and responsibilities in informing and influencing public opinion, providing a forum for the communication and exchange of ideas and opinions, and in holding those in power to account.

Concept of a 'free press/freedom of the press'

A free press, or **freedom of the press**, is a concept that states that for a free, open and democratic society to exist the press should be free from political and judicial interference and be able to print any news stories they wish. Clearly within any society there needs to be laws to protect individuals and organisations from newspapers printing false stories, but restrictions upon the press should be limited. The term 'free press' is now more widely interpreted to mean freedom for any form of **mass media**.

- Television in the UK is governed by legislation that states that it has to be politically impartial; a formal renewable charter governs the operations of the BBC.
- There is no requirement upon newspapers or magazines to be politically impartial. In fact, during elections political parties look to newspapers to support their cause.
- The internet is often referred to as the 'wild west' as there are no distinct laws governing its operation, but individuals and the state can bring legal actions against those who break existing laws via their use of the internet.

> **Freedom of the press** – a concept that states that for a free, open and democratic society to exist the press should be free from political and judicial interference and be able to print the stories they wish.
>
> **Mass media** – communicating to a large audience at the same point in time. Media consists of several different types of communications: television, radio, newspapers, magazines and the internet.

What do we mean by the media?

Traditional media includes the printed format such as newspapers and magazines, and later the cinema, radio and television. Now, in addition, **new media** includes all forms of internet-linked communication. Hence the growth of terms like **e-media** and social media and in the last decade the concept of the **citizen journalist**; individuals who report on situations where they live directly on the internet.

> **Exam tip**
>
> Do not confuse a 'free press' with free newspapers. Free newspapers are newspapers that are given away free of charge.

> **Traditional media** – newsprint, radio, television, cinema.
>
> **New media** – a broad term that emerged in the later part of the twentieth century that relates to the development of internet-related means of communication. New media holds out a possibility of on-demand access to content at any time, anywhere, on any digital device, as well as interactive user feedback, citizen participation and community formation around the media content.
>
> **e-media** – all forms of media related to the internet; 'e' stands for electronic.
>
> **Social media** – this can take many different forms, including internet forums, weblogs, social blogs, Twitter, Facebook, etc., micro-blogging, wikis, podcasts, photographs or pictures, video, rating sites and social bookmarking. These all enable citizens to control their own news agenda without referring to the traditional media.
>
> **Citizen journalist** – where individual citizens act as journalists to gather news and distribute there video footage and commentary via social media and news organisations to a worldwide audience.

What is the role of the media in a modern society?

- **Inform** the public about what is going on and provide information on complex issues in such a way that they are accessible to their readership
- **Encourage** public debates on major issues of public concern
- **Uncover** abuses of power and challenge decision-makers and press for changes
- **Campaign** and create and support public opinion in regard to issues and injustices
- **Speak to power** so that those who hold positions of power (political, economic, social) are both accountable and aware of public opinion and also ensure that a range of political views and opinions are made available to the public.

What are the responsibilities of the media towards society?

- **Ensure** that there is a balance between fact, analysis and opinion when reporting news
- **Work in a professional manner** ensuring their reporting is as accurate as possible
- **React/set the political agenda** by explaining issues to allow the public to understand and participate in the debate
- **Publish corrections** and be **accountable** for what they publish
- **Ensure** that the **public interest** is a priority both what is and what is not published, for example not to print information that could be harmful to national security or endanger individuals.

What must society ensure exists so that there is freedom of the press?

- **Establish** a legal and taxation framework that allows the media to thrive/survive
- **Ensure** that there is a legal and regulatory framework that encourages a range of views (plurality) and addresses issues such as the concentration of media ownership and ownership by non-UK individuals or companies, for example:
  - **make available** the necessary airwaves and infrastructure to allow for a range of media outlets
  - **encourage** both the private media and public media sectors
  - **ensure** that all political parties have access to the media especially during election campaigns
  - **establish** a legal framework that encompasses freedom of information laws but also legislates for privacy to provide a limit to media intrusion
  - **create** a regulatory framework that enables citizens, groups and organisations to hold the media accountable for their actions.

Media impact

It is important to consider today the impact of the various media formats. Social media and news on the internet can by its nature be seen and read and shared by millions of people within minutes. Table 11.1 indicates the declining circulations of national newspapers in the UK. Most of these now also have paid or open online platforms so they can ensure that they operate a 24/7 news service as well as attract advertisers so that their businesses remain profitable.

Table 11.1 Newspaper sales July 1980, July 2011 and January 2017

Newspaper	Party political leanings since 1980	July 1980	July 2011	January 2017
The Sun	Has been both Labour and Conservative	3.7m	2.8m	1.7m
Daily Mirror	Labour	3.6m	1.2m	0.7m
Daily Mail	Conservative	1.9m	2.0m	1.5m
Daily Telegraph	Conservative	1.4m	0.6m	0.5m
The Times	Has been both Labour and Conservative	0.3m	0.4m	0.5m
The Guardian	Labour/Liberal Democrat	0.4m	0.25m	0.15m

Table 11.2 Number of people viewing news bulletins on the TV, June 2017

TV Channel	Viewing figures
BBC1 10 o'clock News	5.49m
ITV	3.13m
Channel 4 News	0.72m
This compares with the two most popular BBC and ITV programmes: 'EastEnders' and 'Coronation Street'	6m

On the social media format Twitter the top two most followed people are Katy Perry with 100,417,176 followers and in second place Justin Bieber with 97,421,312.

On Facebook, which has 1.79 billion users worldwide, the top five shared items in 2016 were:

1 'New Alzheimer's Treatment Fully Restores Memory Function' (5 million shares)
2 'How Sensitive is Your OCD Radar?' (3.4 million shares)
3 'Science Says the First Born Child is the Most Intelligent' (2.8 million shares)
4 'An Open Letter to my Friends who Support Donald Trump' (2.2 million shares)
5 'Bald Men are Sexier, More Masculine, Scientific Study Says' (2.1 million shares)

It is considered that during the 2017 General Election the Labour Party led by Jeremy Corbyn did better than the Conservatives when it came to social media campaigning. This is underlined by the fact that Corbyn's Facebook page saw 4,360,000 engagements from 8 May to 8 June 2017. Theresa May's page saw just 554,000 interactions.

> **Exam tip**
>
> Remember when answering questions about the media to cover a range of differing formats. Also be aware that questions can relate to a specific format, for example the role of the internet or differences between TV and newspaper news coverage; ensure that you relate to the media that the question is focused upon rather than writing generally about them. The data above show how the impact of differing media formats has changed and is still changing.

Holding those in power to account

The media are one of the main ways in which those in power, whether they are politicians or in business, can be held to account. Newspapers, television and the radio all carry out investigative journalism, which can establish the facts of an issue and ensure there is a public debate, often leading to those in power answering to Parliament or the courts.

An example is the Parliamentary expenses scandal exposure by the *Daily Telegraph* in 2009 where MPs had their expenses claims made public. This led to changes in the rules for MPs' expenses, several criminal cases and many MPs not standing at the next General Election. Another example is the publication in 2015 a photograph of a dead child washed up on a beach in Turkey; this led to a public outcry over the UK government's policy on refugees.

The right of the media to investigate and report on issues of public interest

REVISED

In the UK the media have the right to fully investigate and publish news stories they believe to be in the public interest. Those who believe the stories are inaccurate and damage them can use civil law to seek damages from the media. But this is often very expensive and time consuming. The media also have insurances against such costs.

The Freedom of Information Act has given the media as well as members of the public the ability to gather information about the work of public bodies. It is therefore seen as a duty for the media to ensure that their stories are accurate and protect individual privacy where necessary. This is a balancing act between their freedom and their responsibilities. To ensure this balance is maintained the state on behalf of the government and citizens has set out a regulation structure for the media (see below).

Cases where the media has prompted action by its investigative stories include:

- *The Guardian* and how those in the newspaper industry had used phone hacking as a means to gain information.
- The *News of the World* campaigned regarding paedophiles, which led Parliament to pass a law known as 'Sarah's Law'.

The operation of press regulation and examples of where censorship is used

REVISED

The internet is currently not subject to formal legal regulation, although governments around the world are trying to introduce laws and regulations. Some countries ban access to some content and close down the internet completely for periods of time.

Press regulation in the UK is currently in a fluid situation. For a number of years the industry was self-regulatory through the Press Complaints Council but following the phone hacking scandal the government set up a Royal Commission led by Lord Justice Leveson. He recommended in his Report in 2012 that the newspaper industry should continue to be self-regulated and the government should not try to control what papers publish. His ruling states:

- The old Press Complaints Commission (PCC) was not fit for purpose and should be replaced.
- A new body should be established to promote high standards, including the power to investigate complaints and impose penalties.
- This new body should be established by the industry with a new code of conduct.
- This new body should be backed up by legislation designed to ensure that the new body is doing its work properly.

Many newspaper owners and editors did not agree with the recommendations of the Leveson Report and in 2014 established their own independent body the **Independent Press Standards Organisation (IPSO)**. IPSO handles complaints and conducts investigations into standards and compliance. It has the power to require published corrections, and can fine publications. Over 1400 print titles have signed up to IPSO. However, the *Guardian*, the *Independent* and the *Financial Times* have not joined IPSO. It has already adjudicated in over 1000 complaints. IPSO looks at complaints in relation to the Editors' Code of Practice, which is the ethical code under which journalists are expected to work.

> **IPSO** – the Independent Press Standards Organisation is an industry-based body which self-regulates most newspapers in the UK.

The code relates to the following aspects of reporting:

- accuracy
- opportunity to reply
- privacy
- harassment
- intrusion into grief or shock
- children
- children in sex cases
- hospitals
- reporting of crime
- clandestine devices and subterfuge
- victims of sexual assault
- discrimination
- financial journalism
- confidential sources
- witness payment in criminal trials
- payments to criminals.

This code of conduct can be considered a form of self-censorship by the newspaper and magazine industry. Regarding all of these points, journalists should be able to state that the story was in the public interest and so was not in violation of the code. It is often this question of 'in the public interest' that is finally resolved if matters go to a court hearing.

The government has now approved **IMPRESS** as the official press regulator but very few newspapers have signed up to be a part of its regulatory structure. Impress maintains a Standards Code, and assesses any breaches of this code by its members. It also provides an arbitration scheme that is free to the public and protects publishers against the risk of court costs and exemplary damages.

Censorship

Censorship is the ability to suppress or prevent the publication of information. As well as censorship by outside bodies, the press themselves at times exercise self-censorship when they refuse to use materials they are offered either individually or collectively as an industry.

Censorship also exists in relation to other media formats:

- Films are classified as to their suitability for certain age groups by the British Board of Film Classification. If they are not approved, they cannot be shown in British cinemas.
- The Broadcast Advertising Clearance Centre approves all television advertising before it is shown.
- The Advertising Standards Authority (ASA) governs other advertising formats.
- **Ofcom**, a government body, has regulatory powers in regard to the media.

As noted previously, the internet is currently not subject to formal legal regulation, although some governments are trying to introduce laws and regulations. Some countries ban access to some content and close down the internet completely for periods of time. An example of the newspaper industry's self-censorship in the UK was in regard to the use of photographs surrounding the death of Diana, Princess of Wales in a car crash in Paris.

With regard to national security, the government can issue a DSMA-Notice which requests that editors do not report a matter as it is against the national interest. The Terrorism Act 2006 made it an offence to 'glorify terrorism'. Some see this as a limit upon free speech. In 2013, the offices of the *Guardian* newspaper were raided by the police following the publication of stories about surveillance. The stories were based upon leaked material provided by Edward Snowden, a former National Security Agency (NSA) employee in the USA.

IMPRESS – the approved government regulator of the press, however, very few newspapers have joined this body.

Censorship – suppression of materials, publications and thoughts.

Ofcom – Office of the Regulator for Communications. This is the government-established independent regulator and competition authority for the UK communications industries.

The Observer in 2004 kept secret a memo showing that the UK had conducted a potentially illegal spying operation at the UN prior to the Iraq War.

Websites

- UK government: www.gov.uk
- BARB (Broadcasters' Audience Research Board): www.barb.co.uk
- Ofcom: www.ofcom.org.uk
- IMPRESS: http://impress.press
- IPSO: www.ipso.co.uk
- Open Rights: www.openrightsgroup.org/campaigns/censorship – A group that campaigns regarding potential internet censorship
- Newswhip: www.newswhip.com/2017/06/labour-won-uks-social-media-election/ – An account of the social media campaign in the 2017 General Election
- *The Guardian*: www.theguardian.com/media/2015/oct/21/uk-media-plurality-threatened-by-dominant-group-of-large-firms-report – A news story about media ownership in the UK

Now test yourself

TESTED ☐

1 Define what is meant by the term 'censorship'.
2 Name the regulatory body set up by most newspapers' owners in 2014.
3 Explain what is meant by the phrase 'in the public interest' regarding newspaper stories.
4 Identify one way in which the Freedom of Information Act aids journalists.

Answers online

Exam practice

Chinese media control

The Chinese government has long kept a tight control on both traditional and new media to avoid potential challenge to its power and authority. Its tactics often mean strict media controls using monitoring systems and firewalls, shuttering publications or websites, and jailing dissident journalists, bloggers and activists. At the same time, the country's growing economy relies on the web for growth, and experts say the growing need for internet freedom is testing the regime's control.

1 Describe how the situation in the United Kingdom differs from that in China as described in the source. [4]
2 Examine why some people believe that the power of newspapers to influence public opinion is declining. [8]
3* Justify the argument that politicians should pass laws to control and regulate the different forms of media that exist in the UK.
In your answer you should consider:
- the different forms of media that currently exist
- the role of government in protecting its citizens. [8]

ONLINE ☐

12 What is the UK's role in key international organisations?

The role of the UK within international organisations

United Nations (UN)

- The UN was established in 1945 when representatives of 51 countries met in San Francisco, USA, to draw up the **United Nations Charter**. The United Nations officially came into existence on 24 October 1945. This day is now celebrated as United Nations Day.
- The UN has its headquarters in New York, where all member countries meet to decide the policy and actions to be taken by the UN. The General Assembly is the forum to which all member countries belong. The **Security Council** is made up of fifteen members, five of which are permanent and have the ability to **veto** any proposals.
- The UK is a founder member of the UN and has a permanent seat on the Security Council.
- Today the UN is one of the most important international bodies in the world, with 193 members.
- In 1948, after much discussion and debate, the UN adopted the Universal Declaration of Human Rights (UNDHR), which identified rights to which all people are entitled.
- The four purposes set out in the Charter of the UN are:
  1 To maintain international peace and security
  2 To develop friendly relations among nations
  3 To co-operate in solving international problems and in promoting respect for human rights
  4 To be a centre for harmonising the actions of nations.

> **United Nations Charter** – a document that lays down the aims of the United Nations.
>
> **Security Council** – the major decision-making body of the United Nations. Made up of five permanent members and ten elected member countries. The UK is one of the permanent members.
>
> **Veto** – the ability to vote down any decision.

North Atlantic Treaty Organisation (NATO)

- NATO is an intergovernmental military defence alliance. It was established in 1949 and the UK was a founder member. It has its headquarters in Brussels, Belgium. The organisation provides for a system of collective defence – if a member country is attacked, the other members come to its defence.
- There are currently 28 member states of NATO. The most recent countries to become members are Albania and Croatia, which joined in April 2009. Besides European countries, its membership includes the USA, Canada and Turkey.
- NATO also has a number of partnership arrangements with other countries and organisations from the Atlantic to Central Asia and co-operates with a network of international organisations. While NATO has not been called upon to use its members' armed forces to defend their members' borders, it did take command of the UN-mandated International Security Assistance Force (ISAF) in Afghanistan in August 2003. Its mission was to enable the Afghan government to provide effective security across the country and to ensure that it would never again be a safe haven for terrorists.
- NATO's mission was completed at the end of 2014. NATO member countries' combined military spending accounts for over 70 per cent of the world's defence spending. NATO has set a target for member countries to spend 2 per cent of their GDP on defence. Following the 2017 General Election, the new Conservative government pledged to maintain UK defence spending at the 2 per cent target figure set by NATO for the next ten years.
- NATO is now also focused on the worldwide fight against terrorism and is working to counter cyber-terrorism.

European Union (EU)

- The European Union was formerly known as the European Economic Community (EEC) and more usually as the Common Market. The six founding member countries that signed the Treaty of Rome in 1957 were France, West Germany, Belgium, The Netherlands, Luxembourg and Italy.
- The Community aimed to encourage trade between member countries, allow for the free movement of people between countries and work towards 'an ever-closer union'. Sir Winston Churchill first suggested the idea of a United States of Europe in 1946. The EEC was seen as a way of preventing future wars in Europe. Twice in the twentieth century there had been war in Europe, with the six member countries taking opposing sides. In 2017 there are 28 members of the EU, of which 18 used the **Euro** as their currency. The UK joined in 1973, after being refused membership by the French President in 1961 and 1968.
- The headquarters of the EU is divided between Brussels in Belgium and Strasbourg in France.
- In a national referendum in June 2016 the UK voted to leave the EU. In March 2017 the Conservative government led by Theresa May triggered Article 50 of the Lisbon Treaty which started the withdrawal process. This means that the UK will leave the EU by March 2019.
- Negotiations are currently underway regarding how the UK withdraws from the EU and what future relationship the UK will have with the EU, especially in regard to trade matters.
- Currently the UK has 73 Members of the European Parliament (MEPs) out of 751. UK MEPs are elected by the closed regional party list system. Those in Northern Ireland are elected using the single transferrable vote (STV). The UK MEPs will remain in office until the UK leaves the EU.
- The decision-making process within the EU is different from that which operates in its member states. Proposals for new laws, directives or initiatives are drafted by the **European Commission**. These are then considered by the member state governments at **Council of the European Union** meetings. The European Parliament is then consulted.
- Four times a year, heads of government from all the member states meet at the **European Council** to discuss the political direction and priorities of the EU.

Euro – the common currency used by the Eurozone (eighteen members of the EU).

European Commission – appointed officials from member countries of the EU who draft policy initiatives and direct the workings of the EU.

Council of the European Union – meetings of ministers from member states of the EU.

European Council – meetings of the heads of government of EU member states.

Council of Europe

The **Council of Europe** is the continent's leading human rights organisation. Forty-seven countries are members, of which 28 are also members of the European Union. The Council of Europe is not itself a part of the European Union. All member countries agreed to abide by the **European Convention on Human Rights.** The convention was adopted in 1950 and came into force in 1953. The European Court of Human Rights oversees the implementation of the Convention. The Court is made up of judges from all its member countries. The UK was a founder member of the Council of Europe and helped draft the Convention. Individual citizens can bring complaints of human rights violations to the Strasbourg Court, once all possibilities of appeal have been exhausted in the member state concerned. The European Union is preparing to sign up to the European Convention on Human Rights, creating the ability for any of the 508 million citizens within the EU to access the European Court of Human Rights.

The European Convention on Human Rights

The Convention enshrines the basic human rights and fundamental freedoms of everyone within the jurisdiction of any member state. These include rights:

- to life
- to protection against torture and inhuman treatment
- to freedom and safety
- to a fair trial
- to respect for private and family life
- to freedom of expression (including freedom of the press), thought, conscience and religion
- to freedom of peaceful assembly and association.

The UK played a major part in drafting the ECHR and in 1998 incorporated the Convention into UK law via the Human Rights Act (HRA).

> **Council of Europe** – founded in 1949 and is an intergovernmental organisation whose aims are to promote human rights, democracy, and the rule of law within its 47 member states. This body established the European Convention on Human Rights.
>
> **European Convention on Human Rights** – a convention that lays down basic human rights. It is based upon the Universal Declaration of Human Rights (UDHR), and is overseen by the Council of Europe.

Exam tip

Make sure you do not confuse the Council of Europe and the ECHR with the EU. They are two distinct bodies.

Exam tip

You are not expected to become an expert on trade issues, but as you follow the news about the UK's future relationship with the EU, this table will give you an idea to how it links to the government's declared policy indicated in the Lancaster House speech by the Prime Minister.

The Commonwealth

Formerly known as the British Commonwealth, the Commonwealth has 53 member countries, which span Africa, Asia, the Americas, Europe and the Pacific. Thirty-one of the members are small states with fewer than 1.5 million people. The Commonwealth represents about 30 per cent of the world's population. Its members include some the richest and some of the poorest countries in the world. All members must agree with the values set out in the **Commonwealth Charter**. The Commonwealth is a voluntary organisation and its Charter brings together the values that unite the Commonwealth – democracy, human rights and the rule of law. The Head of the Commonwealth is Queen Elizabeth II, and its headquarters are in London. Heads of government of the member states meet every two years at the Commonwealth Heads of Government Meeting (CHOGM).

> **Commonwealth Charter** – a document that lays down the principles associated with Commonwealth membership.

World Trade Organisation (WTO)

The World Trade Organisation came into being in 1955 as the successor body to the General Agreement on Tariffs and Trade (GATT) which was set up at the end of the Second World War. The UK was a member of GATT from 1948 and joined the WTO in 1955. The WTO has 161 member countries and its headquarters are in Geneva, Switzerland. The WTO is the only global organisation dealing with trading rules between nations.

The WTO claims to:
- cut living costs and raise living standards
- settle trade disputes and reduce trade tensions between nations
- encourage economic growth and employment
- cut the cost of doing business
- encourage good governance
- help countries develop
- give the weak a stronger voice
- help support health and the environment
- contribute to peace and stability.

The UK was a founding member of all the organisations mentioned above, except the European Union, and played a key role in their development and work.

Case study: The EU In–Out Referendum: the UK votes to leave the EU

- For the third time in its history all the electors within the UK were able to take part in a referendum. In 1975 the referendum was about the UK membership of the European Economic Community and in 2011 it was about changing the voting system regarding how we elect MPs.
- Following the 2015 General Election, the re-elected Prime Minister David Cameron reiterated a Conservative Party manifesto commitment to hold an 'in–out' referendum on Britain's membership of the European Union by the end of 2017, following renegotiations with EU leaders.
- The referendum took place on 23 June 2016. In the 2015 General Election, the United Kingdom Independence Party (UKIP) – whose main aim is for the UK to leave the European Union – achieved 3.9 million votes (12.6 per cent of the votes cast), but won in only one constituency. However, in the 2014 elections to the European Parliament, UKIP topped the poll, with 27.5 per cent of the vote and had 24 MEPs elected.
- Since the 1990s, the gap between those who wanted to 'stay in' the EU and those who wanted to 'get out' has narrowed significantly. The 1975 Referendum was 2:1 in favour of remaining in the then EEC.
- Both sides of the debate received taxpayer funding to promote their cause. Politicians for different political parties found themselves debating and disagreeing with members of their own parties.
- All the major UK political parties with the exception of UKIP favoured the UK remaining a member of the EU. While the television channels have to be politically neutral the press was divided over membership, with the *Daily Telegraph* supporting a Leave vote and the *Daily Mirror, The Times, The Guardian* and the *Financial Times* supporting a Remain vote.
- The Remain campaign was led by the Prime Minister, David Cameron and the Chancellor of the Exchequer, George Osborne while two of the leading Leave campaigners were also important members of the Conservative party: Boris Johnson and the Justice Minister, Michael Gove.

The result

- Votes to leave: 17,410,742 (51.9%)
- Votes to remain: 16,141,241 (48.1%)
- The turnout was 72 per cent.
- The result showed some interesting voting patterns: In England every counting region with the exception of London voted by a majority to leave the EU.
- The morning after the count the Prime Minister, David Cameron, announced that he was going to resign his office. After a leadership campaign Theresa May, the Home Secretary, became Prime Minister, campaigning on the theme that 'Brexit means Brexit '.

Table 12.1 How the nations of the UK voted in the referendum

Nation	% vote to leave	% vore to remain	% turnout
England	53.4	46.6	73.0
Scotland	38.0	62.0	67.2
Wales	52.5	47.5	71.7
Northern Ireland	44.2	55.8	62.9

Table 12.1 indicates how the UK voted in the referendum. Many who supported UK membership of the EU pointed out the economic benefits to the UK of membership. The Single Market with its 500 million people generates about £10 trillion of economic activity. The EU accounts for half of the UK's overall trade and investments. Around 3.5 million jobs in the UK are linked to our EU trade.

Those who campaigned for a Leave vote claimed that the issues of parliamentary and legal sovereignty were under threat from the EU, a body it said was undemocratic. Their slogan of 'Take back control' encapsulated their campaign.

It is currently unclear what future relationship the UK will have with the EU or what the cost will be to the UK of leaving the EU. Commentators talk of hard or soft Brexit meaning that we could have a free trade arrangement with the single market (soft) or no arrangement so in future we would trade with the EU on World Trade Organization terms (hard).

Table 12.2 sets out the various options that might be available to the UK regarding future trade arrangements with the EU.

Table 12.2 The UK's possible future trade relations with the EU

	PM's Lancaster House Speech	Stay in Single Market but leave Customs Union — Norway	Leave Single Market but negotiate a customs union — Turkey	Leave Single Market and Customs Union but negotiate bilateral trade agreement			Leave single Market and Customs Union with no deal — WTO option
				Switzerland	Ukraine	Canada	
Control migration from the EU	✓	✗	✓	✗	✓	✓	✓
End ECJ jurisdiction	✓	Partial	Mostly	Mostly	Partial	✓	✓
End applicability of EU regulations	✓	✗	Partial	Partial	Very limited	✓	✓
Pursue an independent trade policy	✓	Mostly	Very limited	Mostly	✓	✓	✓
Stop obligatory budgetary contributions to the EU	✓	✗	✓	✗	✓	✓	✓
Exit CAF and CFP	✓	✓	✓	✓	✓	✓	✓
Tariff-free trade with the EU	✓	✓	✓	✓	✓	✓	
Access to the EU Single Market for services	✓	✓	✗	Very limited	✓	Very limited	✗
Seamless and frictionless border, including in Northern Ireland	✓	Partial	Partial	Partial	Partial	✗	✗
Voluntary participation in EU programmes	✓	✓	✓	✓	✓	Partial	✗
Speed of negotiation (within Article 50 process)	✓	✓	✓	✗	✗	✗	N/A

Key points the UK wants to achieve by leaving the EU (rows: Control migration from the EU, End ECJ jurisdiction, End applicability of EU regulations, Pursue an independent trade policy, Stop obligatory budgetary contributions to the EU, Exit CAF and CFP)

What the UK wants from the EU (rows: Tariff-free trade with the EU, Access to the EU Single Market for services, Seamless and frictionless border, Voluntary participation in EU programmes, Speed of negotiation)

The first column indicates the UK government opening position.
The remaining columns move from a soft to a hard Brexit outcome.

How the UK has assisted in resolving international disputes and conflicts

The UK has played an active part in attempting to resolve international disputes and conflicts. The methods used have varied from mediation to humanitarian aid, from the use of sanctions to the use of force. In recent years, the UK government has been involved in trying to resolve a number of international disputes and has worked with international bodies and **agencies** and directly with other nations to help resolve issues. Some of these interventions have been controversial and still divide public opinion in the UK. The UK's intervention in Iraq from 2001 to 2009 was subject to the Chilcot Inquiry which was set up in 2009, after British troops had left Iraq, to investigate the background to British involvement in the Iraq War.

> **Agencies** – organisations and bodies that are a part of a major institution: for example, the UN or EU.

Mediation

The UK has been involved in numerous mediation attempts to resolve disputes and conflicts by seeking a peaceful resolution or sponsoring international conferences which lead to a peaceful resolution. From 1968 until 1998, the history of Northern Ireland was linked to the phrase 'the Troubles'. Several attempts to seek a peaceful solution to the civil unrest and conflict between the opposing Unionist and Nationalist communities had failed. The UK government imposed direct rule from Westminster. The bombing and killing spread from Northern Ireland to the UK mainland. By 1993, a framework had been agreed for a peaceful agreement to the Troubles, based upon the idea of 'consent': that any agreement can only proceed if the people of Northern Ireland consent. In 1996, former US Senator George Mitchell agreed to chair the Northern Ireland peace talks. After all-party talks, an agreement was announced on Good Friday 1998.

This Good Friday Agreement was put to the people of both Northern Ireland and the Republic of Ireland (Eire) in a referendum, and both voted in favour of the agreement, which is still in force today. In this case, it took the influence of an outside but interested party – the USA – to enable an agreement to be reached, which involved the UK government, the government of the Irish Republic and all political parties in Northern Ireland.

Sanctions

The UK government operates a range of sanctions from arms embargoes and trade control restrictions, to defence export policies against a number of countries and terrorist organisations. These sanctions are normally imposed as part of a collective action by international bodies such as the EU, NATO or the UN. In 2015, arms embargoes or controls were being imposed on over 50 countries, ranging from Myanmar (Burma), Syria and Zimbabwe to Belarus and Eritrea. Sometimes sanctions can take the form of boycotts, where citizens and organisations refuse to buy goods or use services relating to a specific country or company to express their opposition to a policy or action. Sometimes the government undertakes a boycott. In 2012, the UK government refused to send a minister to attend the football UEFA European Championship due to the actions of the then Ukraine government.

In the past, groups and citizens boycotted South African goods when the country was run by the apartheid regime. Nestlé, the Swiss-based company, has faced a boycott from consumers because of its policy of selling baby-feeding products in Africa.

Use of force

The UK armed forces have been involved in numerous military actions since 1990. Most of these actions have involved working with others in alliances or the allocation of troops to an international force under the control of an international body like the EU, NATO or the UN. Many of these actions have proved to be controversial. One parliamentary convention that has developed following the Iraq War is that the government should obtain the approval of the House of Commons before committing British troops into action abroad.

On the following occasions since 1991 UK forces have been used abroad:
- **1991** The Gulf War
- **1992–96** UN peacekeeping mission in the former Yugoslavia
- **1998** Operation Desert Fox – a four-day bombing campaign against targets in Iraq
- **1999** NATO-led campaigns in the former Republic of Yugoslavia and Kosovo
- **1999** Part of a multinational peacekeeping force in East Timor
- **2000** Evacuating non-combatants and rescuing captured British troops in Sierra Leone
- **2001–14** Involvement in combat operations as part of a US-led campaign in Afghanistan
- **2003** UN mandated French led crisis management in the Democratic Republic of the Congo
- **2003** Invasion of Iraq (British troops remained in Iraq until 2011)
- **2011** Military intervention in Libya

How non-governmental organisations (NGOs) respond to humanitarian crises

REVISED

Whenever there is a natural disaster or civil war, appeals are made to provide funds to help those in need. Many of these appeals are by single organisations, but they are often made by umbrella groups such as the Disasters Emergency Committee (DEC), which works with a range of **non-governmental organisations (NGOs)** to provide urgent help and relief. DEC works with thirteen leading UK aid charities in times of crisis. Since its launch in 1963, it has run 67 appeals and raised more than £1.4 billion. The UK government is the first country in the G7 to honour the UN target set in 1970 of ring-fencing 0.7 per cent of its GNI (Gross National Income) for international aid spending.

The Department for International Development is responsible for allocating around £12 billion of UK taxpayers' money a year on aid. The Department allocates some funds to the work of the NGOs. The work of NGOs is best studied through case studies of their actual activities. A sample of NGOs is included in the website list below.

> **Non-governmental organisations (NGOs)** – non-profit, voluntary citizens' groups which are organised on a local, national or international level. Task-oriented and run by people with a common interest, NGOs perform a variety of services and humanitarian functions.

Websites

These are the official websites of the organisations named in this chapter:
- United Nations: www.un.org/en
- NATO: www.nato.int
- EU: www.europa.eu/index_en.htm
- Council of Europe: www.coe.int/en
- Commonwealth: www.thecommonwealth.org
- World Trade Organization: www.wto.org

The following is a sample of websites belonging to NGOs:
- United Nations: http://en.unesco.org/partnerships/non-governmental-organizations/list – A worldwide directory of NGOs, not just those involved in humanitarian aid

These are examples of NGOs concerned with humanitarian aid:
- Action Against Hunger: www.actionagainsthunger.org/ – Works to save lives of malnourished children while providing communities with access to safe water and solutions to hunger, food security and livelihoods
- CARE: www.care.org/ – Dedicated to ending poverty, saving lives and achieving social justice
- Doctors Without Borders: www.doctorswithoutborders.org/ – Comprising mainly doctors and health workers who provide assistance to populations in distress and victims of disasters and armed conflict
- International Medical Corps: https://internationalmedicalcorps.org/ – Assists those in urgent need by providing first-response healthcare and healthcare-related emergency services
- Islamic Relief: www.islamic-relief.org.uk/ – Independent humanitarian and development organisation with a presence in over 40 countries across the globe
- International Rescue Committee (IRC): www.rescue.org/ – Humanitarian relief and development organisation founded at the request of Albert Einstein; offers emergency aid and assistance to persons displaced by war, persecution or natural disaster
- International Committee of the Red Cross: www.icrc.org/en/node/1 – Helps people affected by conflict and armed violence and promotes the laws that protect victims of war; mandate stems from the Geneva Conventions of 1949
- International Federation of the Red Cross and Red Crescent Societies: www.ifrc.org/ – Carries out relief operations to assist victims of disasters combined with development work
- Oxfam International: www.oxfam.org/en – Works to create solutions for poverty using sustainable development programmes, public education, campaigns, advocacy and humanitarian assistance
- Refugees International: www.refugeesinternational.org/ – Advocates for lifesaving assistance and protection for displaced people and promotes solutions to displacement crises
- World Jewish Relief: www.worldjewishrelief.org/ – British Jewish community humanitarian agency tackling Jewish poverty, primarily in the former Soviet Union
- World Vision: www.wvi.org/ – Global Christian relief, development and advocacy organisation working with children, families and communities to overcome poverty and injustice

Now test yourself

TESTED

1 Explain why the UK has a veto on decisions at the United Nations.
2 Name the body that drafts policy ideas within the European Union.
3 Identify the reason why NATO was established.
4 Define what is meant by 'soft power'?

Answers online

Exam practice

Civil war in Ukraine

The civil war that broke out in Ukraine has led to the division of the country into two parts, one that leans heavily towards the EU and the eastern part that is closely associated with Russia. As a result of this conflict Russia took over the Crimea, which is a part of Ukraine, and annexed it to become a part of Russia, following a referendum. The EU and the USA have all taken action against Russia because of this annexation.

1 Discuss two possible non-direct military forms of intervention the EU can take that might make Russia reconsider its position. [4]

2 Examine what is meant when politicians say they favour either a 'hard or a soft Brexit'. [8]

3* Many people argue that the UK should not spend 0.7 per cent of its GDP on overseas aid but should instead spend the money on public services in the UK.
Evaluate both points of view.
In your answer you should consider:
● how the UK overseas aid budget is spent
● UK public services and how they are funded. [8]

ONLINE

13 What laws does a society require and why?

Remember, the first section of each of the themes outlines the major concepts and introduces elements that are followed up in greater depth and developed in the other parts of the Theme.

The fundamental principles of law to ensure rights and freedoms

The system of law used in the United Kingdom is based upon a number of key concepts that revolve around the central idea of the 'rule of law', which is a doctrine whereby every person, no matter who they are, is subject to the law, and every person should be treated equally.

This concept incorporates the principles outlined in Table 13.1.

Table 13.1 Principles of the 'rule of law'

Key principle	Definition	Commentary
The idea of legal certainty	This means that all laws in the UK must be applied in a precise and predictable manner.	Everyone must be able to know that their conduct is regulated by the law in a certain manner.
That laws are properly enacted and clear in their purpose	That the UK's formally agreed processes enact laws and that the purpose of any law is clearly set out.	Within a democracy it is important that laws are enacted by due process and also that laws are clear in their intention.
That there is equality and fairness	**Equality before the law** is about the law treating every person equally, allowing every person equal access to the justice system. Fairness relates to treating people equally and appropriately according to the circumstances. Two people from differing circumstances who each commit the same offence for the first time should not be dealt with differently.	The law applies to every individual in society equally. Even members of the royal family have appeared in court and been convicted of motoring offences. The legal system should treat everyone equally and not provide unfair access to the law to anyone. Those charged and found guilty of an offence should not be treated differently.
That laws cannot be retrospective: that is, you cannot be charged with something that is now an offence that you carried out before the law came into force	Legislation cannot be pre-dated so that someone finds that an action they took prior to the legislation is now unlawful and they are charged with the new offence.	People need to know that if they are obeying the law as it currently stands they cannot be charged for taking action if in future it becomes unlawful.
That there is due legal process	The judicial system operates as laid down in law and contains certain **rights**: to a fair trial, to defend oneself, to be represented, (if found guilty) to appeal.	This is an important guarantee of a citizen's rights and is fundamental to the operation of our justice system.

Equality before the law – the principle that any person, regardless of their income, wealth, social or celebrity status, or political power or influence, is treated the same way in regard to the law and the ways in which it operates.

Rights – these are moral, ethical or legal principles that are considered as the basis of the values that underpin a society. For example, the term human rights relates to those values that are guaranteed by society to an individual: the right to vote, the right to free speech, the right to a fair trial.

Exam tip

There is no requirement to know the specific wording of these principles, you need to be aware of them and be able to outline an understanding of how they are interconnected.

There is also a range of other concepts, terms and expressions that relate to the way our justice system operates. Table 13.2 outlines some other building blocks of our legal system that have developed as a result of the nature of 'the rule of law'.

Table 13.2 Legal system terms

Term	Definition	Commentary
Justice	This is a concept based upon our behaviour or treatment relating to what is morally right and fair. There are differences of opinion between different countries and societies about what justice is. Each country's justice system is based upon a system of moral values which can differ from one country to another.	This is an overarching concept that underpins our understanding of the legal and judicial process. It implies so many related ideas such as fairness, equality and due process.
Presumption of innocence	Within our legal system it is assumed that a person who is brought before a court is presumed innocent and it is up to the state to prove their guilt beyond reasonable doubt rather than the accused having to prove their innocence.	This is a basic principle within our legal system. Some systems assume guilt and it is up to the accused to prove their innocence.
Trial by jury	An early principle of English justice was that people accused of a crime should be judged by their 'peers', that is people of equal standing from their community. The jury hears the evidence and on that basis following a summing up by the judge makes a decision about guilt or innocence	Traditionally juries have had to reach unanimous verdicts about the guilt of an accused. In recent years the idea of a majority verdict has been introduced to stop any attempt at bribing or threatening members of the jury. A jury asks a judge if they will accept a majority verdict, they can allow at most a vote of 10 to 2.
Access to justice	This principle relates to the ability of any individual citizen to access and use the justice system irrespective of their status or wealth within society.	Many argue that while in general terms the UK system upholds this principle many changes have been made regarding legal aid especially in regard to civil law cases, where wealth can give access while poverty does not guarantee access.

The nature of our justice system has been described as follows:

'The purpose of the criminal justice system is to deliver justice for all, by convicting and punishing the guilty and helping them to stop offending, while protecting the innocent. It is responsible for detecting crime and bringing it to justice; and carrying out the orders of court, such as collecting fines, and supervising community and custodial punishment.'

Source: An extract of a presentation by Jon Collins, Campaign Director of the Criminal Justice Alliance, to the Centre for Parliamentary Studies, 18 May 2010

Presumption of innocence – a fundamental principle of English law whereby a person charged with an offence is assumed innocent until found guilty in a court of law. This presumption of innocence ensures state must convince the court that the person is guilty beyond reasonable doubt. It is not up to the person accused to prove their innocence.

From a citizenship rather than a purely legal aspect, an important part of the rule of law concept is that within a democracy, it is ultimately based upon the consent of the people and reinforced by the involvement of ordinary citizens in the operation and decision-making processes within the justice system.

Citizen involvement:

- **Members of a jury** – randomly selected citizens determine the outcome in many trials. This role is seen as a very important citizenship duty.
- **Magistrates** – ordinary citizens can volunteer to serve as Magistrates (Justices of the Peace – JPs). Magistrates determine most minor criminal cases in the Magistrates' Courts.

The nature of rules and laws in dealing with fairness, justice and discrimination

REVISED

This section relates to the **rules** and **laws** that a society needs to help it deal with the complex problems of **fairness**, **justice** and **discrimination**. The key words fairness and justice have already been discussed so what do we mean by discrimination? This relates to how we treat others. This can be about individuals or groups of people. You are discriminating against them if you treat them differently based for example upon their age, gender, sexuality, race, disability, and so on, except where the law allows.

In order to resolve past issues of unfairness and discrimination governments have tried a range of policies to counter these issues, but in many cases Parliament has decided to pass legislation making issues relating to unfairness, injustice and discrimination unlawful and punishable by the courts.

This section deals with rules as well as laws. The term rules is used in relation to the way a group or organisation operates while laws relate to the way in which society is regulated. For example, in 2017 the Muirfield Golf Club was banned from holding the Open Championship because it did not allow females to become members. After a second vote, a majority voted in favour of changing its membership rules.

Examples of antidiscrimination legislation passed in the United Kingdom include:

- Race Relations Acts 1965, 1968, 1976 and 2000
- Equal Pay Act 1970
- Sex Discrimination Acts 1975 and 2002
- Disability Discrimination Act 1995 and 2005
- Equality Acts 2006 and 2010

> **Rules** – regulations or statements that govern behaviour within a specific area of activity. For example, a school has rules not laws, the rules of football do not apply to Rugby Union.
>
> **Laws** – the system of formulated ideas of how members, groups and bodies within a society should behave and be regulated. Each society will have its own means of determining its laws, which are recognised as regulating the actions of its citizens and others in the country and which if not obeyed can lead to the imposition of penalties.
>
> **Fairness** – impartial and just treatment for all people; behaviour without any form of favouritism or discrimination.
>
> **Justice** – behaviour or treatment that is morally right and fair.
>
> **Discrimination** – treating a person or group of people unfairly on the basis of their sex, gender, race, etc.

Exam tip

There is no requirement to know the specific dates and nature of each piece of antidiscrimination legislation. The important Act is the Equality Act 2010, which created what is now the Equality and Human Rights Commission that has responsibility for enforcing the legislation. The 2010 Equality Act merged all the previous legislation into the new Act.

Rights in local to global situations where there is conflict and where rights and responsibilities need to be balanced

In situations from the local to the global there are often conflicts, meaning disagreements, about rights and responsibilities which then need need to be re-balanced temporarily or permanently. This can happen where a new form of government takes over a society and takes citizens' rights away or where a situation occurs that forces those in authority to make changes. Within a democracy those who make the changes are eventually accountable to the electorate who can vote to put forward their view about the changes.

Different societies, cultures and countries can have differing views on some legal issues. For example, the death penalty was abolished in the UK but it is still used in other countries. In the USA, it is fairly easy to obtain a gun, and the country has a very high death rate from gun violence, whereas in the UK there are very tight controls over gun ownership.

Following the end of Second World War in 1945 and the establishment of the United Nations, it was decided to try to establish agreement on common human rights for all people. This led to the Universal Declaration of Human Rights being drafted. It was added to and in 1976 gained the standing of International Law. Currently 192 countries have signed the Declaration.

The Council of Europe further devised the European Convention on Human Rights. The UK played a major part in its drafting and was one of the original signatories in 1950. Currently 47 countries have signed the Convention. Many members of the Council incorporated the Convention into their constitutions. In 1998, the UK formally wrote the Convention into UK law via the Human Rights Act.

There has to be a balance between the power of the state and the rights and duties of its citizens. At times, this balance is brought into question. These are some case study examples of the rights versus responsibilities conflict.

- In the UK the police have powers of 'stop and search', but many ethnic minority community members complained that they were subject to the use of these powers more than other groups. This eventually led to the government changing the guidance on the use of stop and search.
- After the 9/11 terrorist attacks in New York, new security measures were introduced at airports. This was done with public approval. In 2017, the USA decided to impose a ban on carrying computer equipment as cabin luggage; this has not had the same level of public support, even though it has been introduced on security grounds.
- In Northern Ireland in the 1970s, judges decided the outcome of cases as it was not possible to hold jury trials.

An example of countries working together to assist crime fighting can be seen by others as undermining their rights. For example, the European Arrest Warrant allows a UK police force to ask for the arrest of a citizen of another country for a crime they are alleged to have committed in the UK. On receipt of the UK paperwork the local police force will arrest the citizen and deport them to the UK. This speeds up the justice process but does not allow the accused the right of full access to their own country's legal system to stop the deportation.

> **Exam tip**
>
> This is a topic where it is very helpful to have a case study to quote as through case studies you can demonstrate both knowledge and understanding.

Increasingly citizens look to international agreements to assert their rights. The **European Court of Human Rights** in Strasbourg is used by many citizens to help resolve their rights when they are in dispute with authorities in their own countries. In 2017 the Court ruled in favour of a group of Russian citizens regarding how the Russian government and its forces ended a siege at a school in Beslan when terrorists had taken 1000 hostages. In total, 330 civilians, many children, died as a result of the Russian armed forces storming the building. The Court found that the Russian government had not taken sufficient precautions based on prior information about the terrorists and that they used undue force to end the situation. The Russian government says that the ruling is 'utterly unacceptable' and that it would appeal.

> **European Court of Human Rights** – Court of the Council of Europe that sits in Strasbourg and rules on the European Convention on Human Rights. It must not be confused with the European Court of Justice, which is the court of the European Union.

Websites

- Equality and Human Rights Commission: www.equalityhumanrights.com – An independent statutory body with the responsibility to encourage equality and diversity, eliminate unlawful discrimination and protect and promote the human rights of everyone in Britain; the Commission enforces equality legislation on age, disability, gender reassignment, marriage and civil partnership, pregnancy and maternity, race, religion or belief, sex and sexual orientation
- European Court of Human Rights: www.coe.int/t/democracy/migration/bodies/echr_en.asp – The European Court of Human Rights is an international court set up in 1959; it rules on individual or state applications alleging violations of the civil and political rights set out in the European Convention on Human Rights
- Universal Declaration of Human Rights: www.un.org/en/universal-declaration-human-rights – This United Nations website gives full details of the content of the Declaration and its historical setting in the post-Second World War period
- European Convention on Human Rights: www.echr.coe.int/Documents/Convention_ENG.pdf – This website makes available a full copy of the Convention in English
  https://rightsinfo.org/the-rights-in-the-european-convention/ – This website offers a full copy of the Convention with a useful commentary and points to consider
- Huffington Post: www.huffingtonpost.com/bryan-stevenson/tremaine-mcmillian-case_b_3560827.html – This is the complete article from the exam practice source

Now test yourself

TESTED ☐

1 Define what is meant by the expression 'the rule of law'.
2 Explain how a rule differs from a law.
3 Name the body that oversees the Universal Declaration of Human Rights.
4 Identify which of the following Acts of Parliament linked all existing antidiscrimination legislation together:
   a Race Relations Act
   b Disability Discrimination Act
   c Equality Act
   d Equal Pay Act

Answers online

Exam practice

Being presumed guilty is frustrating, burdensome and exhausting. In the criminal justice system it can also be dangerous and life threatening. When police, prosecutors or judges presume someone's guilt, lives are destroyed and horrific injustices take place. We need to talk about this problem in the United States.

Source: Bryan Stevenson, Huffington Post, 8 July 2013

1 Describe how the justice system in the United Kingdom takes a different view than that indicated in the source. [4]

2 Examine the view that a citizen has both rights and responsibilities within society. [8]

3*Evaluate the arguments made in favour of the media being able to fully report on all court cases taking place in the United Kingdom.
   In your answer you should consider:
   ● the current ability of the media to report court cases
   ● the nature of different types of court cases heard in the United Kingdom. [8]

ONLINE

14 What are a citizen's rights and responsibilities within the legal system?

The operation of the justice system

REVISED

The justice system contains five sub-parts, all of which relate to the workings of the system:

1 the police
2 the **judiciary**
3 legal representatives
4 **criminal** and **civil law** courts
5 tribunals and dispute resolution.

> **Judiciary** – the part of the UK system of governance that is responsible for its legal system and that consists of all the judges in its courts of law.
>
> **Criminal law** – the type of law where individuals are charged by the state with an offence and if found guilty are punished by the state.
>
> **Civil law** – the type of law that deals with disputes between individuals where damages are awarded.

1 The role and powers of the police

This element breaks down into two components:

- What is the role of the police?
- What are the powers of the police?

The role of the police

The role and responsibilities of the police as laid down in the police service's Statement of Common Purpose is as follows: 'The purpose of the police service is to uphold the law fairly and firmly; to prevent crime; to pursue and bring to justice those who break the law; to keep the Queen's peace; to protect, help and reassure the community; and to be seen to do this with integrity, common sense and sound judgement.'

Another way of considering the role of the police is to think about their core operational duties, which include:

- protecting life and property
- preserving order
- preventing the commission of offences
- bringing offenders to justice.

The police have additional duties that are laid down under legislation and **common law**.

> **Common law** – law based upon judges' rulings in court.

When considered from the position of an individual police constable the role, as outlined by the Scottish Police, broadens the work of the police giving it a community focus:

- work alongside communities, liaising with community groups and individuals
- provide a visible presence to deter crime and reassure the community
- conduct patrol duties on foot, by car and bicycle
- develop community knowledge to identify individuals and locations at risk of being involved in crime
- respond to calls and requests from the public to assist at incidents
- keep the peace at public meetings, social events, processions, trade disputes or strikes
- diffuse potentially volatile situations with due regard for the safety of all involved
- act with sensitivity when dealing with situations such as delivering news of a sudden death or when dealing with sexual crimes
- conduct initial investigations, gather evidence, take statements and comply with relevant legal requirements

- interview suspects, victims and witnesses in accordance with relevant legislation
- conduct arrests with due regard for the human rights, security and health and safety of detained individuals, members of the public, colleagues and self
- prepare crime reports and present case files to senior officers and the Crown Prosecution Service (CPS) (England and Wales), the Crown Office and Procurator Fiscal Service (COPFS) (Scotland), or the Public Prosecution Service for Northern Ireland (PPS)
- attend and give evidence in court and at other hearings
- complete administrative procedures

- submit internal crime reports and criminal intelligence reports
- investigate and take action on information received from members of the public
- gather, record and analyse intelligence to achieve community safety and crime reduction objectives and provide crime prevention advice
- take direction on specific duties from senior colleagues
- attend road-related incidents including collision scenes, vehicle check points and traffic offences
- enforce road traffic legislation and issue fixed penalties for relevant offences
- deal with lost or found property.

The powers of the police

Table 14.1 The most commonly used powers of the police

Police power	Commentary
Stop and search	A police officer has powers to stop and search if they have 'reasonable grounds' to suspect a person is carrying illegal drugs, a weapon, stolen property or something that could be used to commit a crime, such as tools.
Power of arrest	In order to arrest someone the police need reasonable grounds to suspect they have been involved in a crime for which an arrest is necessary. The police have powers to arrest anywhere and at any time, including on the street, at home or at a workplace. When arresting a person the police procedure is to: • identify themselves as the police • tell the person that they are being arrested • tell the person what crime the police think has been committed • explain why it is necessary to make the arrest • explain that the arrested person is not free to leave. If the person to be arrested is under 17 the police should only arrest them at school if it is unavoidable, and they must inform the head teacher. The police must also contact the parents, guardian or carer as soon as possible after the person arrives at the police station.
Entry, search and seizure	In certain circumstances set out in the Police and Criminal Evidence Act 1984 (PACE), the police have the power to enter premises and search them to either arrest someone, seize items in connection with a crime, or both. Police usually need to obtain a warrant from the court before they can enter and search premises. There are situations, however, when the police may enter premises to search them without a warrant. The police may seize anything that is on a premises if they have reasonable grounds for believing: • that it has been obtained in consequence of the commission of an offence • that it is necessary to seize it in order to prevent it being concealed, lost, damaged, altered or destroyed.

From a citizenship perspective it is also important to understand that in the UK unlike other countries there is no national police force. The police service is operated on a regional basis as it is the aim that the police should have local accountability. There are 43 distinct police forces in the UK. Scotland and Northern Ireland each have a single police force. The **Metropolitan Police Force** in London does provide some national services to the other police forces. Today, with the exception of the two London-based forces, each police force has a directly elected Police and Crime Commissioner. Within each police force day-to-day operations are the responsibility of the Chief Constable who is accountable to their Police and Crime Commissioner. In London, the Mayor shares police oversight with the Home Secretary. Police forces also employ **police and community support officers** to assist the public and help prevent antisocial behaviour.

> **Metropolitan Police Force** – the title of the police force that is responsible for the London area. It is often referred to as 'the Met'.
>
> **Police and community support officers** – local employed uniformed staff who help the police in local communities. They do not have police powers.

2 The role and powers of the judiciary

Table 14.2 The different roles within the hierarchy of the judiciary

Lord Chief Justice	The most senior judge in the UK: the head of an independent judiciary
President of the Supreme Court	Head of the UK's highest domestic appeal court
Justices of the Supreme Court	Judges who hear civil and criminal appeals in the UK's most senior court
Senior President of Tribunals	Head of the judges in the UK Tribunal Service
Master of the Rolls	President of the Court of Appeal (Civil Division)
Chancellor of the High Court	Head of the Chancery Division of the High Court
President of the Family Division	Head of Family Justice
President of the Queen's Bench Division	Also Deputy Head of Criminal Justice
Lord Justices of Appeal	Hear appeal cases in the civil and criminal divisions of the Court of Appeal
High Court Judges	May hear trial and appeal cases in the High Court, sit on some appeals in the Court of Appeal and judge serious cases in Crown Court trials
Circuit judges	Hear criminal cases in Crown Courts and civil cases in the County Courts
Recorders	Work part-time hearing criminal cases in the Crown Court and civil cases in County Courts; they are qualified barristers or solicitors
District judges	Hear the bulk of civil cases in the County Courts
District judges (Magistrates' Court)	Deal with the most complex cases in a Magistrates' Court
Tribunal judges	Deal with most cases brought before tribunal hearings; they often sit with lay members
Magistrates	Volunteers from the local communities who agree to sit and dispense justice in Magistrates' courts. Also referred to as Justices of the Peace (JPs). They receive training and are supported by legal advice in the courtroom. They normally sit as a 'bench' of three magistrates. By 2022 it is projected that there will be only 12,000 Magistrates; as recently as 2009 there were 30,000 and currently there are about 18,000

Now test yourself and exam practice answers at **www.hoddereducation.co.uk/myrevisionnotes**

The role of the judiciary is to administer justice according to the law, pass sentences in criminal cases and make decisions in civil law cases. With the exception of Magistrates all other positions listed in Table 14.2 are filled by professional trained lawyers and most of the posts are full time and salaried.

Table 14.3 The role of judges

The role of judges	Commentary
Preside over court proceedings	A judge ensures that a court case follows agreed rules and through their expertise advice on points of law. They also give guidance to a jury on the evidence and points of law.
Interpret and apply the law	A judge has to interpret the law as drafted by Parliament and apply it to the case under consideration.
Create case law	Where the law is unclear, judges have to make rulings; once these are upheld or used by other courts they become judge-created 'case law'.
Decide sentencing	A judge determines the sentence following a jury decision. The amount of discretion a judge has regarding the sentence is now limited as sentencing policy is often laid down by law.
Chair public inquiries and commissions	Judges undertake this role because they are seen as independent and impartial. Inquiries are organised and run along the lines of a court hearing. The Leveson Inquiry into the role of the media was a judge-led inquiry.
Protect the citizen from an overbearing state	If a citizen has a grievance about the power of the state the judiciary is an independent body that can adjudicate.

Powers of the judiciary

Judges play many roles and these roles allow them to exercise a range of powers; they have the power to interpret the law and to control hearings and trials in their courtrooms. Most important of all, following a decision by a jury, they alone have the power to determine the sentence given. Increasingly the range of sentences for specific offences is laid down within legislation so judges have limited room for manoeuvre. In the statements they make in court judges do have the power to influence debate and discussion on specific topics. In almost all civil cases judges sit alone so determine the merits of the evidence and decide the outcome of the cases and any award made.

3 The roles of legal representatives

The three main branches of the legal profession are: **legal executives**, **solicitors** and **barristers**. A way of recalling their roles is to think about your health: the legal executive is the paramedic, the solicitor is the family doctor, and the barrister is the hospital consultant.

Many people, especially those with limited means and if the issue is a civil dispute, will visit their local **Citizens Advice** office and seek free legal advice.

Legal executives – legally qualified specialists employed largely by solicitors.

Solicitors – mainly graduates who cover a range of both civil and criminal legal work and have to be formally qualified.

Barristers – graduates who become specialist in a narrow aspect of the law and are employed by solicitors on behalf of their clients to represent them in the higher courts.

Citizens Advice – community-based charity that provides help and advice, including free legal advice throughout the UK.

Queen's Counsel – barristers may apply to become QCs (KCs if there is a king on the throne). This is recognition by their profession that they have become experts in their own field.

Table 14.4 The roles of the legal representatives

Legal representative	Commentary
Solicitors	Solicitors undertake most of the work in Magistrates' Courts and County Courts, both in the preparation of the case and its advocacy. They also deal with a large amount of commercial work, land and building issues and the conveyancing of houses, making wills and advising on tax matters.
	Many are graduates with a law degree. They must undertake professional training of a one-year legal practice course and then two years under training in a solicitor's practice. They are regulated by the Law Society.
Barristers	Barristers' traditional work has been advocacy. They present cases in court. A barrister is briefed (employed) by a solicitor to work on the solicitor's client's behalf. Barristers are independent of the solicitor and pursue their own judgement about how to proceed with the case. They can work in a Magistrates' Court, but they mainly work in Crown Courts, the High Court or in the appeal court. They are normally specialists in a specific area of law, either civil or criminal. Most barristers are law graduates and they have to undergo training by undertaking the Bar Vocational Course and then pupillage (on-the-job training) with a qualified barrister.
	Most senior barristers apply to become **Queen's Counsel (QCs)**. Barristers work for themselves, but often shares premises, known as chambers, with other barristers.
Legal executives	Legal executives are legally qualified professionals employed largely by solicitors and normally specialise in a given area of law. They are regulated by the Institute of Legal Executives.

4 How the different criminal and civil courts work

The Structure of the Courts

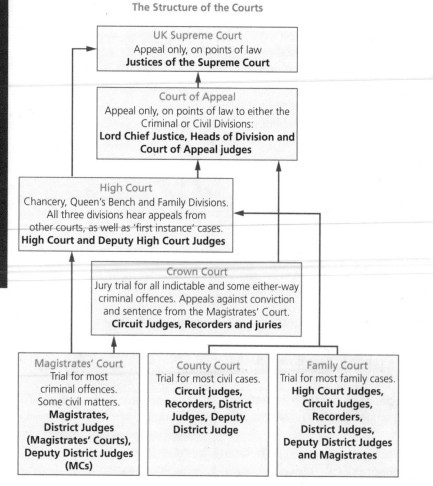

Figure 14.1 The court structure in England and Wales

Now test yourself and exam practice answers at **www.hoddereducation.co.uk/myrevisionnotes**

Figure 14.1 shows that the criminal and civil court system is interlinked. Magistrates' Courts and Crown Courts deal mainly with criminal cases. County and Family Courts deal with civil cases.

Table 14.5 indicates how the progress of civil and criminal cases through the courts differs.

Non-custodial – a criminal sentence that does not involve imprisonment.

Custodial – a sentence that involves imprisonment.

Table 14.5 Differences between criminal and civil processes

Element of the process	Criminal Courts	Civil Courts
The Court Case	The Crown Prosecution Service decides whether a case is brought on behalf of the state.	The case is brought by an individual, group or organisation.
Decision	The defendant is convicted if guilty or acquitted if not guilty. The decision is made by a jury or magistrates.	The defendant is found liable or not liable (responsible) in regard to the issue.
Level of proof required	Beyond reasonable doubt.	Preponderance of evidence. Evidence must be produced to support the claim.
Burden of proof	The accused is innocent until proven guilty. The prosecution must prove their case; the accused does not have to prove their innocence.	The claimant must give proof of the claim.
Sanctions	A **non-custodial** or **custodial** sentence is given if found guilty.	Compensation is awarded or an injunction (an order to stop taking an action) granted.
Appeal	The defendant may appeal a court's verdict in regard to either the verdict or the sentence. It is now possible for the state to ask for the sentence to be reviewed.	Either party can appeal a court's decision.

5 Tribunals and other means of dispute resolution

Tribunals are 'inferior' or minor courts in that what happens at a hearing is a judicial process. Those hearing the case can be laypersons and/or legally qualified persons. The decisions made by tribunals can be subject to review by the court system. Tribunals are specialist courts each dealing with specific issues, such as employment or health. The hearings are more informal and complainants often represent themselves.

Ombudsmen refer to official bodies established either by government or approved bodies to investigate complaints. A Parliamentary Ombudsman and a Local Government Ombudsman have been established by law to investigate complaints from the public. They are fully independent and normally their reports are public documents.

Table 14.6 covers the key points about the work of tribunals and ombudsmen.

Table 14.6 Tribunals and ombudsmen

	Details	Advantages	Disadvantages
Tribunals	Tribunals are inferior courts. They deal with a large number of cases each year. A variety of subjects are dealt with by specialised tribunals. These include employment, health and social care, pensions and finance and commerce.	Can deal with specialised issues. Simple and informal procedure. Can be cheaper than conventional courts. Can be quicker than the court system.	Applicants who pay legal professionals to represent them tend to be more successful which possibly highlights inequality for those who cannot afford this option. Reasons for decisions reached are not always clear.
Ombudsmen	An ombudsman is an official who is appointed to check on government activity on behalf of an individual citizen and to investigate complaints that are made. This can be in a range of areas, such as health service, local government, legal services and housing.	The problem may be solved. Can lead to recommended changes made to government agencies or public bodies.	Their powers are constrained by the fact that they cannot deal with matters that could be dealt with by courts. Complaints must be made through an elected representative and so this can be a barrier to citizens wishing to scrutinise government actions.

In the last few years the government has encouraged the use of a system called Alternative Dispute Resolution (ADR) to help citizens with the legal process. Many citizens find accessing the legal system both daunting and expensive. ADR is intended as a way of enabling people to represent themselves in less formal surroundings and achieve a speedy outcome to their case.

Table 14.7 sets out the advantages and disadvantages of various types of ADR.

Table 14.7 The advantages and disadvantages of ADR

Type of Alternative Dispute Resolution	Details	Advantages	Disadvantages
Negotiation	The parties involved discuss issues and compromise or make a decision about how the issues can be resolved.	Very informal No cost Private	The parties involved may not be able to make a decision or compromise.
Mediation	The parties discuss disputes with a neutral third party known as a mediator. The mediator does not disclose their own opinion but instead acts as a facilitator who helps the parties reach their own agreement.	Much cheaper than courts. The parties reach their own agreement so it is likely to last longer than settlements that are forced on them.	The process may not lead to a settlement. The process is not binding.
Conciliation	A conciliator is used to help to resolve disputes but plays a more active role than a mediator, e.g. they might suggest grounds for a possible compromise.	Much cheaper than litigation. It is entirely private. Good success rate.	The process may not lead to a settlement and so parties may have to litigate anyway. It can put pressure on claimants to settle in employment cases and mean that they might accept a lesser settlement than a tribunal would award.

➡

Type of Alternative Dispute Resolution	Details	Advantages	Disadvantages
Arbitration	Arbitration is the process where parties agree to have their dispute heard by a private arbitrator who will make a binding decision. Many commercial contracts contain clauses which say the parties will use arbitration to settle any disputes.	Can be cheaper than courts. Decisions are binding and can be enforced by courts. Parties can choose their own arbitrator. Quicker than court proceedings.	No state funding for arbitration. Professional arbitrators' fees can be high, so may be as expensive as courts. Using professional arbitrators and lawyers might cause delays similar to those experienced in the court system.

Exam tip

The term 'role' often appears in the specification and in examination questions. It is a short-hand phrase for stating what is the position, purpose or function of someone or something in a situation, organisation or society.

Rights and legal entitlements of citizens at differing ages

REVISED

There are a vast number of rights and responsibilities that citizens acquire at different ages. Table 14.8 shows some of the more important rights and the ages at which they are acquired. Historically, 21 was seen as the age when a person reached adulthood and acquired full legal rights. In recent decades young people have acquired more rights at earlier ages, for example the right to vote at 18 (it had previously been 21). In 2016 in Scotland the voting age was lowered to 16 for the Referendum on Scottish Independence. The three major stepping stones for rights are now 16, 18 and 21.

Table 14.8 Rights and the ages they are acquired

Age	Rights
8	Age of criminal responsibility in Scotland
10	You can choose your own religion
	Age of criminal responsibility in England and Wales
12	You can watch a 12 or 12A film or play a 12 category computer game
	You can be remanded into a secure unit or secure training facility for persistent offending
	Age of criminal prosecution in Scotland
13	You can have a part-time job, with some restrictions
	You can have an account on a social networking site like Facebook or Twitter
14	You can enter a pub if the landlord allows it, but you cannot buy or drink alcohol, only soft drinks
15	You may be remanded to a prison to await trial
	If you are convicted of a criminal offence you can be fined up to £1000 and sentenced to prison time
16	You can work full time if you have left school, have a National Insurance number and the job has accredited training
	You can give consent and have sex
	You can be married or live together with a parent's permission
	You can be prosecuted for having sex with someone who is under 16
	You can apply for your own passport with a parent's consent

Age	Rights
17	You can hold a driver's licence and apply for a motorcycle licence
	You can be interviewed by the police without an appropriate adult being present
18	You have reached the age of majority (that is, you are an adult!)
	You can have a tattoo or body piercing
	You can watch an 18 film or play an 18 computer game
	National minimum wage entitlement increases
	You can get a debit card and credit card
	You can change your name
	You can vote and be called for jury service
	You can buy and drink alcohol in a bar
	You can get married, enter a civil partnership or live together without parental consent
	You can stand as an MP or a local councillor
21	You can drive certain types of larger vehicles such as lorries or buses (with the appropriate licence)
	You are entitled to full national minimum wage
	You can apply to adopt a child
	You can get certain types of jobs, for example become a driving instructor
	You can apply for a licence to fly commercial transport, aeroplanes, helicopters, gyroplanes and airships

Exam tip

Focus on a few rights at the key ages that indicate an increasing sense of gaining responsibility within society.

How civil law differs from criminal law

REVISED

It is helpful when revising this element of the course to refer back to the section earlier in this chapter: How the different criminal and civil courts work (see page 106).

Table 14.9 Differences between civil law and criminal law

Civil law	Criminal law
Civil law deals with disputes between individuals such as debt or divorce.	Criminal law deals with individuals and groups who are accused of breaking the law with activities such as theft, violence or riot.
Civil law is about determining on the balance of evidence whether damages should be awarded to the claimants, the person bringing the case or in the case of a divorce have the conditions required by law been meet so that a divorce can be granted.	Criminal law requires the state to prove beyond reasonable doubt that the person charged committed the offence.
In a civil case damages are awarded to the claimant if the case is found in their favour.	In a criminal case a non-custodial or a custodial sentence is given if the person is found guilty.

Now test yourself and exam practice answers at **www.hoddereducation.co.uk/myrevisionnotes**

How the legal systems differ within the UK

Due to the history of the United Kingdom three slightly differing legal systems operate here. Within this book unless stated differently the text refers to legal practice in England and Wales. Table 14.10 indicates how the structure of the courts in Northern Ireland and Scotland differ from England and Wales.

Table 14.10 The legal systems in Northern Ireland and Scotland

Northern Ireland	Scotland
The UK **Supreme Court** hears appeals on points of law in cases of major public importance.	In Scotland, there is also the Court of Sessions, which is the highest court, dealing with civil law cases. In 2015, the Sheriff Appeal Court was established to hear appeals from the Sheriff and Justice of the Peace Courts. The hearings take place before two or three appeal sheriffs. Since 2016 they also deal with civil case appeals.
The Court of Appeal hears appeals on points of law in criminal and civil cases from all courts.	The High Court deals with the most serious cases such as murder, rape and armed robbery. Cases are presided over by a single judge and tried by a jury of fifteen people.
The High Court hears complex or important civil cases and appeals from the County Court.	Sheriff and jury: cases are heard by the sheriff and a jury of fifteen jurors (members of the public). A Sheriff Court can impose a custodial sentence of up to five years.
County Courts a wide range of civil actions including Small Claims and family cases.	Sheriff and summary: the sheriff (judge) determines guilt or innocence as well as presiding over the trial. They can impose a custodial sentence of up to one year and impose a fine of up to £10,000.
The Crown Court hears all serious criminal cases.	Justices of the Peace act in a similar fashion to the Magistrates' Court system in England and Wales.
Magistrates' Courts (including Youth Courts and Family Proceedings) hear less serious criminal cases, cases involving juveniles and civil and family cases.	
Coroners' Courts investigate unexplained deaths.	
The Enforcement of Judgments Office enforces civil judgments.	

> **Supreme Court** – the final court of appeal in the UK for civil cases, and for criminal cases from England, Wales and Northern Ireland. It hears cases of great public or constitutional importance affecting the whole population.

Websites

- Scottish government: www.gov.scot – The website of the Scottish government, which gives details of all aspects of government in Scotland
- Scottish government: http://www.gov.scot/publications/2017/03/5915/6 – A government website outlining courts Reform
- Courts and Tribunals Judiciary: www.judiciary.gov.uk – An official UK government website regarding the operation of the legal system
- Crown Prosecution Service: www.cps.gov.uk – A government website outlining the work of the CPS
- Police.UK: www.police.uk – The national police portal for information about policing in the UK; each individual police force has its own website.
- nidirect government services: www.nidirect.gov.uk/articles/introduction-justice-system – The website of the devolved authority in Northern Ireland, which gives details of all aspects of government in the province
- The Law Society: www.lawsociety.org.uk – The official website of the body that represents solicitors
- The Bar Council: www.barcouncil.org.uk – The official website of the body that represents barristers
- Chartered Institute of Legal Executives: www.cilex.org.uk – The official website of the body that regulates legal executives

Now test yourself

TESTED

1 Explain the main role of the Crown Prosecution Service (CPS).
2 Define what is meant by 'case law'.
3 Identify a legal right you are given at the age of 18.
4 What is the name of the highest civil court of law in Scotland?

Answers online

Exam practice

A nine-year-old boy was arrested and charged with criminal damage and appeared without legal representation in a Magistrates' Court. The Magistrates remanded the boy in custody and referred the case to the Crown Court.

1 With reference to the case above consider how it could be claimed not to conform to the requirements of the law in England. [4]
2 Examine the case for **or** against all police officers in the UK automatically carrying firearms. [8]
3* In some countries members of the judiciary are directly elected by voters or appointed by political parties.
Justify a case why the UK is correct not to adopt this approach to appointing members of the judiciary. In your answer you should consider:
- the current way members of the judiciary are appointed
- how the notion of political appointments conflicts with the principles underpinning the UK legal system. [8]

ONLINE

15 How laws protect the citizen and deal with criminals

How citizens' rights have changed and developed over time

REVISED

From Magna Carta, 1215 there began the development of basic **legal rights:**
- the right to a free trial
- the use of juries
- not being arrested without reason.

From this grew a call for **political rights** with major changes taking place in the nineteenth and twentieth centuries with the right to vote. Woman did not get the right to vote until 1918, when they could vote at the age of 28, and they only got the vote at 21 in 1928. The voting age was lowered from 21 to 18 in 1971.

Campaigns regarding **religious rights** continued into the nineteenth century. Male Roman Catholics were only given the vote in 1829, and in 1832 the first major reform of who could vote and the size and distribution of parliamentary seats took place.

As the UK became an industrial society in the nineteenth century, campaigns took place to develop **economic rights** – for example, the right to form and join a trade union. In 1834, some farm labourers from Dorset, known as the Tolpuddle Martyrs, were sent as convict prisoners to Australia because they swore an illegal oath on joining an agricultural workers' trade union.

In the twentieth century, the idea of **welfare rights** developed in the UK. Citizens now have an expectation that certain services and benefits are provided for everyone – for example, education, health care, pensions and unemployment benefit.

In recent years, **rights** relating to a citizen's **personal** life have become the basis for changes in law – for example, equal opportunities legislation, equal pay and issues relating to sexuality such as homosexual law reform and the concept of civil partnership and equal marriage rights.

There are currently growing calls in regard to rights concerning **global issues and environmental issues.**

Figure 15.1 How rights have developed since Magna Carta

Figure 15.1 indicates how over time the concept of rights has developed. Magna Carta is used as a first pillar in the development of rights in the United Kingdom. The nature of the demand for rights has changed over time and in regard to some aspects of rights there are demands for more changes.

Case study: The right to vote

In the example of political rights:
- women only fully achieved the right to vote in 1928
- in 1968 the voting age was lowered to 18 from 21
- in 2014 the voting age for the Scottish independence referendum was lowered to 16
- in the 2017 General Election some political parties campaigned for the voting age for all elections to be lowered to 16.

Exam tip

There is no requirement to know the full details of Magna Carta (the Great Charter) of 1215, just to understand how it challenged the concept of power and authority at the time.

The 1998 Human Rights Act (HRA) came into force in 2000:
- It codified all existing UK human rights legislation and while it did not extend existing human rights, it did ensure that they were embraced within a single Act.
- This Act also ensured that the European Convention on Human Rights was embedded in UK law.
- This meant that UK citizens could bring cases before UK Courts and have them resolved without having to go to the European Court of Human Rights in Strasbourg.
- It also meant that UK courts had to abide by and take account of decisions of the Court in Strasbourg when arriving at their own decisions.

Contemporary issues

Politicians on the right of the political spectrum have called for a British Bill of Rights to replace the HRA and the European Convention on Human Rights. They believe that the court is assuming powers and authority in areas beyond the original scope of the Convention and they are also concerned about the composition of the courts that make the decisions.

> **Exam tip**
>
> Do not confuse the European Convention on Human Rights and the European Court of Human Rights in Strasbourg with the European Union. They are two very different bodies. The Convention and Human Rights Court are a part of the Council of Europe that has nothing to do with the European Union. The European Union has its own court, the European Court of Justice (ECJ), which meets in Luxembourg. It can be confusing because the European Parliament meets in Brussels and Strasbourg.

Common law, legislation and how they differ

REVISED

Table 15.1 Common law, legislation and how they differ

Common law	Legislation	Difference commentary
Basic definition: law that has developed as a result of rulings made by judges in court cases.	Basic definition: also known as statute law. These are Acts of Parliament that set the will of Parliament in regard to an area of life and may include the prescription of sanctions or punishments.	Common law can be adjusted with time and helps redefine laws that are unclear or are being interpreted for the first time. Lawyers will refer to the latest ruling to assist them preparing cases. Statute law is static until it is amended or superseded by a new law passed by Parliament.

An example of how the two types of law can operate

Parliament may pass a new Road Traffic Act that states that driving while under the influence of drugs is a criminal offence. A person may be charged with this offence and their lawyers will look at any previous judgments to see whether any aspect of the law has been clarified. For example, the issue may be about a driver who is taking a combination of prescribed drugs. If the law is unclear the driver might challenge the charge and ask the judge to clarify the situation. The judge's clarification then becomes case law, which can be used by others in future. If the case progresses to higher courts other judges can make fresh decisions that either dismiss the earlier case law or support it. If Parliament believes this case law undermines their original intention regarding the law they can change the law.

The right to representation; the role and history of trade unions and employers' associations

Representation in this context is about how people join together in mutual support to achieve mutually agreed aims. This element of the course is only concerned with the role of trade unions and **employers' associations**.

> **Employers' association** – industry or regionally based bodies that seek to represent the interests of groups of employers.

The history of trade unions

- **1799 and 1800** The Combination Acts make virtually all trade union activity illegal and subject to three months' imprisonment by the Justices of the Peace
- **1824** Combination Acts repealed
- **1825** New Combination Act restricts union activities
- **1834** Trial of Tolpuddle Martyrs from Dorset; they were agricultural workers who were charged with taking a secret oath to form a trade union and were transported to Australia as punishment
- **1837** First of the Tolpuddle Martyrs return to England
- **1851** Amalgamated Society of Engineers formed; the first of the 'New Model' unions that had members from a range of industries
- **1868** First meeting of the Trades Union Congress in Manchester
- **1870** National Union of Elementary Teachers (later National Union of Teachers) founded
- **1871** Trade Union Act allows Registrar of Friendly Societies to register trade unions and provides a legal basis for their activities and protection for their funds; Criminal Law Amendment Act makes picketing a criminal offence
- **1875** Conspiracy and Protection of Property Act legalises picketing once again
- **1876** Trade Union Amendment Act protects union funds
- **1888** **Strike** by match girls at Bryant & May factory in London's East End
- **1901** Taff Vale judgment makes union funds liable for damages caused by strikes
- **1906** Trade Disputes Act reverses Taff Vale judgment
- **1926** General strike over wage cuts in mining industry: Royal Commission appointed in response to the defeat of attempts to cut wages – the government responds by calling in troops and volunteers to break the strike; TUC issues order to return to work on 12 May
- **1972 and 1974** Miners' strike
- **1978–79** Winter of discontent sees many public sector disputes
- **1980** Trade union membership peaks at 13 million
- **1980–93** Six Employment Acts restrict industrial action by requiring pre-strike ballots, outlawing **secondary action**, restricting picketing and giving employers the right to seek injunctions where there is doubt about the legality of action

> **Strike** – the withdrawal of one's labour; refusing to work.
>
> **Secondary action** – when a worker not directly involved in a trade dispute takes action to support other workers.

As can be seen from this timeline the history of trade unions in the UK has been one of restrictions being put in place and then later removed as the role of the unions became more important in society. The membership of trade unions has been in decline but it still has a very high membership within public services.

Trade unions were formed to represent their members, engaging in negotiations with employers on issues such as wages, safety issues, redundancy and pensions. Some trade unions are affiliated to the Labour Party and give the party financial support. The Labour Party was established by the trade unions.

Employers' associations

Employers' associations are the mirror image of trade unions; they represent the owners of specific sectors of the economy. They seek to influence government and often negotiate as a body with trade unions regarding pay and conditions. In recent years they have been very active representing their interests within the European Union and many belong to pan-European employer organisations.

The following are some examples of employer organisations:
- Association of British Orchestras: www.abo.org.uk
- British Amusement and Gaming Trades Association: www.bacta.org.uk
- Construction Plant Hire Association: www.cpa.uk.net
- Federation of Master Builders: www.fmb.org.uk
- Lancashire Textile Manufacturers' Association: www.ltma.co.uk
- Malt Distillers Association of Scotland
- National Farmers Union: www.nfuonline.com
- Retail Motor Industry Federation Limited: www.rmif.co.uk
- Scottish Decorators' Federation: www.scottishdecorators.co.uk
- Road Haulage Association: www.rha.org.uk
- University and Colleges Employers Association: www.ucea.ac.uk

This government website lists all employer organisations in the UK: www.gov.uk/government/publications/public-list-of-employers-associations-listed-and-unlisted/employers-associations-current-list-and-schedule.

Some are national bodies, others are regional. They seek to represent the interests of their members. The following link provides a directory of pan-European Groups and Associations that operate across a number of European countries: https://www.pita.org.uk/what-we-do/pita-directory/2016-06-15-04-52-59/pan-european-groups-associations.

Case study: The Federation of Window Cleaners

The Federation was established in 1947 as an independent, non-profit-making organisation to support the needs of window cleaners in the UK. Owned by and run only for the benefit of our members.

Our purpose is to maintain and improve the window cleaning industry and to represent our membership, updating our image in line with the unrivalled federation that we have become today and in turn we continue to re-evaluate the service offering we supply to our membership.

Source: Taken from their website: www.f-w-c.co.uk

Now test yourself and exam practice answers at **www.hoddereducation.co.uk/myrevisionnotes**

The nature of criminality in the UK today

Differing types of crimes

While in everyday conversation we use language to describe differing crimes like stealing or attacking someone, official government statistics and measures of crime use a set number of terms to categorise differing crimes.

- **Violent crime** – violence against the person; this can range from murder, manslaughter or knife attack to common assault.
- **Hate crime** – any criminal offence that is perceived by the victim or any person to be motivated by hostility or prejudice, based upon race, religion/faith, sexual orientation, disability or gender.
- **Sexual offences and intimate personal violence**. These are recorded as two groups:
  - rape
  - other sexual offences.
- **Robbery** – an offence in which force or the threat of force is used either during or immediately prior to theft or attempted theft.
- **Theft offences** – these involve burglary, offences against vehicle owners, theft from the person, bicycle theft, shoplifting and all other theft offences.
- **Criminal damage and arson** – defined as intentional or malicious damage to the home, other property or vehicles.
- **Fraud** – an act of deception intended for personal gain or to cause a loss to another party and includes things like using another's credit card and internet and insurance deception.
- **Antisocial behaviour** – includes nuisance, rowdy or inconsiderate neighbours, vandalism, graffiti and fly posting, street drinking.
- **Environmental damage** – includes littering, dumping of rubbish and abandonment of cars, prostitution-related activity, begging and vagrancy, misuse of fireworks, inconsiderate or inappropriate use of vehicles.
- **Other crimes** – includes drug offences, possession of weapons and public order crimes.

Government statistics about crime come from two sources: those recorded by the police, and the Crime Survey for England and Wales (CSEW).

- Police **recorded crime** figures are restricted to a subset of notifiable offences that have been reported to and recorded by the police. Therefore, while the police recorded crime series covers a wider population and a broader set of offences than the CSEW (for example, residents of institutions, tourists and crimes against commercial bodies), it does not include crimes that do not come to the attention of the police or are not recorded by them.
- The CSEW figures are based upon face-to-face surveys asking people in England and Wales about their experiences of a range of crimes in the past year. The survey interviews both adults and children. The CSEW provides a better reflection of the extent of crime than police recorded figures as the survey asks about crimes that are not reported to or recorded by the police. The survey is also unaffected by changes in police recording practices or levels of public reporting to the police.

> **Recorded crime** – crimes that are reported to and recorded by the police.

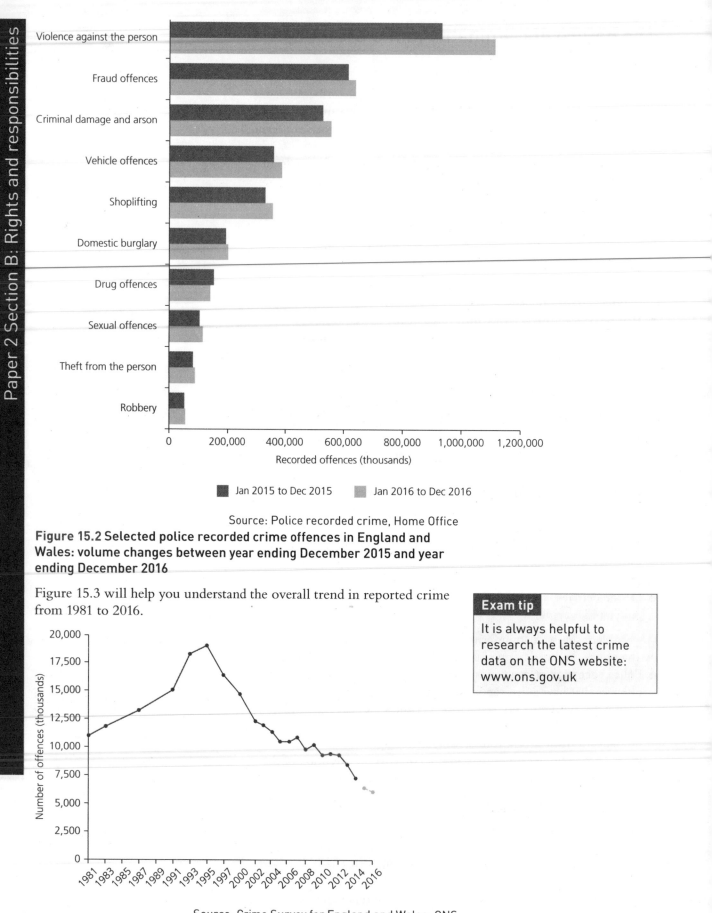

Source: Police recorded crime, Home Office

Figure 15.2 Selected police recorded crime offences in England and Wales: volume changes between year ending December 2015 and year ending December 2016

Figure 15.3 will help you understand the overall trend in reported crime from 1981 to 2016.

Exam tip

It is always helpful to research the latest crime data on the ONS website: www.ons.gov.uk

Source: Crime Survey for England and Wales; ONS

Figure 15.3 Trends in reported crime from 1981 to 2016

Profile of criminality in the UK

In 2012, a government-sponsored report entitled Prisoners' Childhood and Family Backgrounds looked at the past and present family circumstances of 1435 prisoners sentenced in 2005 and 2006.

Its key findings were:
- 24 per cent stated that they had been in care at some point during their childhood.
- 29 per cent of prisoners had experienced abuse or had observed violence in the home (41 per cent) as a child.
- 37 per cent of prisoners reported having family members who had been convicted of a non-motoring criminal offence, of whom 84 per cent had been in prison, a young offenders' institution or borstal.
- 18 per cent of prisoners stated that they had a family member with an alcohol problem, and
- 14 per cent with a drug problem.
- 59 per cent of prisoners stated that they had regularly played truant from school, 63 per cent had been suspended or temporarily excluded, and 42 per cent stated that they had been permanently excluded or expelled.

The Home Office research paper on youth crime showed that youngsters commit a 'disproportionate' amount of crime, as under-18s make up a tenth of the population but are responsible for 23 per cent of offences.

In 2012 the Ministry of Justice produced a report that stated that 24 per cent of people sentenced by a court were female and 76 per cent were male.

The chart below indicates the age of offending, showing that 17 is the peak age for offending.

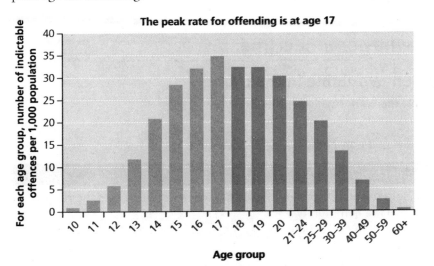

Figure 15.4 Peak age of offending

Factors affecting crime rates in society and strategies to reduce crime

While some people have questioned how crime rate statistics are gathered in the UK, especially those by the different local police forces, this element of the course is concerned with societal issues. Looking at the previous section, clearly family background and educational performance can impact upon the likelihood of criminality.

- If 17 is the peak age for committing crime, is this linked to peer-group pressure?
- Some crime patterns are linked to the state of the economy; if it is in decline and there are high levels of employment there can be an increase in criminality.
- Events can trigger short-term increases in crime. If there are riots and public disturbances there is likely to be an increase in public order offences.
- Motoring offences can appear to increase if the police take a more pro-active approach, for example increasing the use of cameras for detecting offences.
- Also the extent to which the offender believes that the police will successfully apprehend them can have an impact on the crime rate as well as the extent to which the public take additional precautions regarding their property.

Strategies to reduce crime can be at a state level; new laws and punishments can be introduced that impact on criminal behaviour. The state may focus on an aspect of criminality and make funds available to support a pro-active programme like Prevent, which is intended to stop the radicalisation of some members of the community. Some are introduced by the private sector, for example insurance companies will encourage home and motor vehicle owners to consider additional security and will reward them with lower premiums.

Local police forces and local councils encourage the development of Neighbourhood Watch Schemes where local communities are encourage to look after each other and work with the police to prevent and detect criminals.

How we deal with those who commit crime

REVISED

Differing forms of punishment available in the UK

In the criminal justice system in the UK there are two categories of punishment: custodial and non-custodial.

Table 15.2 Differences between custodial and non-custodial sentences

Category	Sentence	Commentary
Custodial – imprisonment	Prison	Offenders normally serve half their sentence in prison, and the rest on licence in the community. If they break the conditions of their licence, they can be sent back to prison.
	Life sentence	Must be given to those found guilty of murder. The judge sets a minimum term before the Parole Board can consider release.
	Extended sentence	A person can be released on licence for up to eight years.
	Determinate sentence	Fixed term in prison. Early release on licence depends upon behaviour.
	Suspended sentence	Sentenced up to two years but carries out a court order such as unpaid work; or receives treatment for drugs or alcohol to avoid serving the time in prison.

→

Category	Sentence	Commentary
Non-custodial – doesn't involve imprisonment	Community service	Community service sentences both punish, through activities such as unpaid work removing graffiti, and try to help people stay out of trouble through, for example, treatment for drug addiction.
	Fine	Fines are for less severe offences and are the most common type of sentence. The amount of fine is set by the court after considering the seriousness of the offence and how much money the offender has.
	Ancillary orders	These impose upon the person conditions relating to their behaviour. Examples include: ● Drink banning order ● Compensation order ● Restraining order ● Football banning order
	Discharge	These are used for the least serious offences for which the experience of being taken to court is thought to be punishment enough. But a discharge can come with conditions that mean the offender must stay out of trouble.

The purposes of sentencing

The Criminal Justice Act of 2003 stated that there were five purposes of sentencing.

Exam tip

Remember that the term punishment relates to criminal offences; damages are awarded in a civil case.

Table 15.3 The five purposes of sentencing

1 Punishing the offender	By taking away the liberty of the offenders or inhibiting their freedom or costing them money, society and the individual can see a punishment taking place.
2 Deterrence	By punishing someone it makes others think about committing crime and thereby acts to reduce further crime.
3 Rehabilitation of the offender	The punishment allows the criminal to reflect upon their offending and change their behavior.
4 Protection for the community	By punishing criminals, especially where imprisonment is involved, those in the community gain a sense of security.
5 Reparations by the offender	The court may force the criminal to meet, or hear the views of, those affected by their actions and may be ordered to make payments to them.

The effectiveness of differing types of sentence

The issue of effectiveness can be measured in regard to repeat offences.
● If a person is sentenced and then does not commit another offence it can be claimed that the sentence is very effective.
● There is no absolute measure or number that says something is effective or is not effective.
● Statistics can include first-time offenders who might indicate a lower chance of repeat behaviour as against a person who has been sentenced several times before and may have a higher chance of repeat behaviour.
● Often the media and pressure groups will use annual figures to pursue a specific point of view.

Listed below are some examples of statistics from the government about the effectiveness of sentences.

Deterrence – use of sentencing to prevent the offender and others committing the offence.

Rehabilitation – an aim of sentencing seeking to change the behaviour of the offender.

Reparations – where an offender has to pay towards the damage they have caused

- In 2011–12, 81,594 out of 107,688 criminals jailed in England and Wales had served a prior community sentence. The Centre for Crime Prevention, a campaign group, states that community sentences fail to stop re-offending.
- Community sentences involves working for a set number of hours doing voluntary work in the community. The footballer Wayne Rooney was sentenced to 100 hours community service for a drink driving offence and as a part of his sentence he had to paint benches. The sentence can also involve drug and mental health treatment. Campaign groups claim that these sentences don't work and that those convicted should be given stiff prison sentences to protect the public. Figures also show that 35% of adults given a community sentence re-offend within 12 months

Another pressure group states that the government needs to extend statutory rehabilitation to the 45,000 short-sentenced offenders released from prison every year, who have the highest reoffending rates and yet currently receive no supervision after release.

According to government figures:
- The overall proven reoffending rate is 25 per cent.
- Adult offenders have a proven reoffending rate of 24 per cent.
- Juvenile offenders have a proven reoffending rate of 38 per cent.
- Adults released from custody have a proven reoffending rate of 44.1 per cent.

These figures fluctuate up and down by a few percentage points over the years.

Nearly 3,000 serious offences committed by reoffending criminals last year

Ministry of Justice figures show that in 2011–12 over 75% of people sent to prison had at least one previous community sentence. The Centre for Crime Prevention claim this shows that community sentencing is a failure and doesn't stop re offending.

Community sentence can involve between 40 and 300 hours unpaid work in the community such as cleaning up graffiti, they can also include programmes of help for those with mental health issues and drug addiction problems. According to the same pressure group 'stiff prison sentences protect the public and have lower re-offending rates'. Data also shows that 35% of adults given a community service order re-offend within 12 months.

These statistics and quotes indicate how difficult it is to arrive at a clear judgement on the issue of effectiveness.

How the youth justice system operates

There are two aspects to consider:
1 The organisation and structure of the Youth Justice Board
2 The operation of Youth Courts

The Youth Justice system deals with people aged 10–17.

1 Youth Justice Board

The Youth Justice Board for England and Wales (YJB) is a body set up by the government. It works closely with **youth offending teams (YOTs)**. The Board oversees and supports the performance of the youth justice system regarding its main aim which is to prevent children and young people from offending. The YJB provides national co-ordination, guidance and monitoring of locally managed YOT partnerships. It is responsible for commissioning secure accommodation for young people who have been sentenced or remanded by the courts.

2 The Youth Court system

When a young person is charged with an offence, they will appear before the Youth Court. If the case cannot be dealt with immediately, the court will make a decision as to whether the young person will be bailed or remanded into custody. If a young person pleads not guilty, a date will be set for the trial when the magistrates will hear all the evidence and decide whether or not the young person is guilty. If the decision is guilty, they will then decide on the most appropriate sentence. If the case is very serious, the Youth Court will send the case to the Crown Court for trial and/or sentence.

A Youth Court is made up of three magistrates or a district judge. There is no jury in this court. The parents or the guardian of the accused must attend if the accused is under 16 years old. Figure 15.5 indicates the informal nature of the court and identifies those who attend.

> **Youth offending teams (YOTs)** – a partnership of organisations (including the police) with a legal responsibility to prevent offending and reduce reoffending. YOTs involve community volunteers in their work and help to develop skills to engage with young people.

A Witness
B Magistrates
C Clerk of the court
D Lawyers for the prosecution and defence
E Defendant
F Parent
G Youth offending team worker
H Usher

Figure 15.5 A Youth Court in session

Websites

- Trades Union Congress: www.tuc.org.uk – This is the national body to which a number of trade unions belong and makes a useful starting point when researching the history and work of trade unions
- Unite: www.unitetheunion.org – An example of a website belonging to one of the largest UK trade unions
- Office for National Statistics: www.ons.gov.uk/ – Official government website for all statistics about the UK
- Sentencing Council: www.sentencingcouncil.org.uk www.sentencingcouncil.org.uk/about-sentencing/types-of-sentence/ – The body responsible for reviewing the application of sentences; it has useful background regarding differing sentences
- Youth Justice Board for England and Wales: www.gov.uk/government/organisations/youth-justice-board-for-england-and-wales/about – The body that oversees the Youth Justice system in England and Wales
- Government National Statistics: https://www.gov.uk/government/statistics/youth-justice-annual-statistics-2014-to-2015 – Publishes important youth crime and justice statistics for England and Wales each year
- NACRO: www.nacro.org.uk – A pressure group concerned with the welfare of those in prison
- The Howard League for Penal Reform: www.howardleague.org – A pressure group that campaigns for penal reform in the UK

Now test yourself

TESTED

1 Explain the term 'common law'.
2 Define what is meant by the term 'rehabilitation'.
3 Name the national body that has oversight of young people who commit crime.
4 Identify one of the two types of sentences given out by judges.

Answers online

Exam practice

1 Figure 15.5 on page 123 shows those involved in a Youth Court. Compare how the composition of the Court above differs from that of a Magistrates' Court. [4]
2 Justify the case for increasing the resources given to help those released from prison. [8]
3*Analyse why in a democracy Parliament needs to pass laws about how trade unions operate.
   In your answer you should consider:
   - the role of trade unions
   - how and why Parliament has passed laws about trade unions. [8]

ONLINE

16 Universal human rights

The importance of key international agreements and treaties in regard to human rights

REVISED

The United Nations Universal Declaration of Human Rights

The **United Nations Declaration of Human Rights (UNDHR)** 1948 is the key legislation in regard to the development of human rights. It is made up of 30 elements.

1 We are all born free and equal.
2 Don't discriminate.
3 The right to life.
4 No slavery.
5 No torture.
6 You have rights no matter where you go.
7 We are all equal before the law.
8 Your human rights are protected by law.
9 No unfair detention.
10 The right to trial.
11 We are always innocent till proven guilty.
12 The right to privacy.
13 Freedom of movement.
14 The right to seek a safe place to live.
15 Right to a nationality.
16 Marriage and family.
17 The right to your own things.
18 Freedom of thought.
19 Freedom of expression.
20 The right to public assembly.
21 The right to democracy.
22 The right to housing, education and child care and help if you are old or ill.
23 Rights to a job, a fair wage and membership of a trade union.
24 The right to rest from work and to relax.
25 Food and shelter for all.
26 The right to education.
27 Copyright protection of your ideas and inventions.
28 A fair and free world.
29 Responsibility: we have a duty to other people, and we should protect their rights and freedoms.
30 No one can take away your human rights.

> **United Nations Declaration of Human Rights** – the UN General Assembly adopted the United Nations Declaration of Human Rights (UNDHR) in December 1948 and for the first time there was an agreed statement of the rights to which all human beings are entitled.

> **Exam tip**
>
> It is not necessary to know every single article. Try to remember a few to quote to be able to show understanding of the extent of the charter.

The European Convention on Human Rights (EHCR) 1953

The European Convention on Human Rights (formerly the Convention for the Protection of Human Rights and Fundamental Freedoms) came into force in September 1953. The Convention and the Court are a part of the structure of the Council of Europe.

The Convention ensured the rights stated in the UNDHR came into effect in European countries, and established an international court with powers to find fault against states that do not fulfil their undertakings. The court sits in Strasbourg, France, and is made up of judges from each of the member countries. The UK was one of the first countries to agree to the ECHR and played a key role in the drafting of the Convention. The Convention has been updated several times since 1953.

- Article 1: Obligation to respect human rights
- Article 2: Right to life
- Article 3: Prohibition of torture, inhuman and degrading treatment
- Article 4: Prohibition of slavery and forced labour
- Article 5: Right to liberty and security
- Article 6: Right to a fair trial
- Article 7: No punishment without law
- Article 8: Right to respect for private and family life, home and correspondence
- Article 9: Freedom of thought, conscience and religion
- Article 10: Freedom of expression
- Article 11: Freedom of assembly and association
- Article 12: Right to marry
- Article 13: Right to an effective remedy
- Article 14: Prohibition of discrimination

> **Exam tip**
>
> It is helpful in regard to the Convention to be able to recall a few recent examples of UK cases that have been heard by the court, for example cases relating to the right to die, prisoners voting or extradition cases. DO NOT confuse this Court, which is a part of the Council of Europe, with the European Court of Justice, which is the court of the European Union.

The UN Convention on the Rights of the Child

The **United Nations Convention on the Rights of the Child** was signed in September 1990 and all members of the United Nations with the exception of the USA have ratified the convention. In total 54 articles make up the Convention. The Convention became a part of UK law in 1992. It places a duty on governments in regard to the following relating to children:

- The right to life.
- The right to his or her own name and identity.
- The right to be protected from abuse or exploitation.
- The right to an education.
- The right to have their privacy protected.
- The right to be raised by, or have a relationship with, their parents.
- The right to express their opinions and have these listened to and, where appropriate, acted upon.
- The right to play and enjoy culture and art in safety.

> **UN Convention on the Rights of the Child** – in 1989, governments worldwide agreed to adopt the UN Convention on the Rights of the Child (CRC). The Convention stated the basic rights in regard to children; what a child needs to survive, grow, participate and reach their potential. The Convention applies equally to every child, regardless of who they are, or where they are from.

Within the UK in recent years governments have established formal Children's Commissioners to protect and enforce the rights of children (see website **www.childrenscommissioner.gov.uk**).

The Human Rights Act 1998

The Human Rights Act 1998 ensured that the European Convention on Human Rights was embedded in UK law. This meant that UK citizens could bring cases before UK courts and have them resolved without having to go to the court in Strasbourg. It also meant that UK courts had to abide by and take account of decisions of the Court in Strasbourg when arriving at their own decisions. It also stated that UK public bodies had to abide by the Convention.

The role of international law in conflict situations

REVISED ☐

How international humanitarian law protects victims of conflict and helps establish the rules of war

International humanitarian law (IHL) aims to:

- protect people who are not involved or are no longer involved in hostilities: the sick and wounded, prisoners and civilians
- set out the rights and obligations of those involved in the armed conflict.

Two important Conventions that underpin the way victims are protected and the conduct of war are the **Geneva Conventions** and the **Hague Convention**.

The Geneva Conventions

Established after the Battle of Solferino in 1864 to help those involved in and those wounded in the battle, the Convention was extended in 1906 and 1929. In 1949 its scope was further extended to include protection for civilians following the experiences of the Second World War. It was extended again in 1977 and 2005 to include land mines and biological weapons and the protection of children in armed conflicts. The International Red Cross is seen as the guardian of the Convention.

The Hague Conventions

This Convention relates to the conduct of war and dates from 1899. It was added to in 1907.

International Criminal Court

At the end of the Second World War, the Allies set up the Nuremberg and Tokyo trials where individuals and organisations were charged with war crimes, crimes against peace and crimes against humanity. In the 1990s, International Criminal Tribunals for the former Yugoslavia and for Rwanda were set up by international agreement. In 1998, 120 countries signed the Rome Statute, which established a permanent **International Criminal Court (ICC)**. The court sits at The Hague in Holland. To date, the ICC has opened a number of investigations regarding alleged abuses in the Democratic Republic of the Congo, the Central African Republic, Uganda, Sudan, Kenya and Libya.

> **International humanitarian law** – a body of law associated with international disputes and the conduct of war and people affected by war.
>
> **Geneva Conventions** – the most important Convention relating to how civilians and others should be treated during a time of war.
>
> **Hague Conventions** – deal with the rules governing the conduct of war.

> **International Criminal Court** – set up in 1998 to try persons indicted for crimes against humanity or war crimes. In all, 120 nations have agreed to work with the Court.

Points to remember

- Human rights are based on key documents such as the UNDHR.
- In the UK, the HRA (1998) is the key document, outlining a citizen's basic human rights.
- UK citizens have the right to appeal their case to the European Court of Human Rights.
- Rights have developed over time, and at different periods in our history different types of rights have emerged to take prominence in public debate.

Websites

- British Institute of Human Rights: www.bihr.org.uk–UK-based charitable organisation that provides up-to-date information about human rights and details of many case studies
- United Nations: www.un.org/en/universal-declaration-human-rights/–This is the portal for accessing all you need to know about the work of the United Nations
- UNICEF: www.unicef.org–Use this website to find out about the work of the United Nations Children's Fund; it also contains details of many contemporary case studies
- UN Office of the High Commissioner: www.ohchr.org–The website of the Office of the United Nations High Commissioner for Human Rights (OHCHR)
- Amnesty International: www.amnesty.org.uk–The world's largest and most influential human rights organisation; their researchers help uncover and stop human rights abuse across the globe
- Human Rights Investigations: http://humanrightsinvestigations.org–A UK-based charitable organisation that aims to answer the need for objective and thorough human rights investigations
- International Committee of the Red Cross: www.icrc.org–An impartial, neutral and independent organisation whose exclusively humanitarian mission is to protect the lives and dignity of victims of armed conflict and other situations of violence and to provide them with assistance
- Equality and Human Rights Commission: www.equalityhumanrights.com–An independent statutory body with the responsibility to encourage equality and diversity, eliminate unlawful discrimination and protect and promote the human rights of everyone in Britain: the Commission enforces equality legislation on age, disability, gender reassignment, marriage and civil partnership, pregnancy and maternity, race, religion or belief, sex and sexual orientation
- European Court of Human Rights: www.echr.coe.int–An international court set up in 1959, it rules on individual or state applications alleging violations of the civil and political rights set out in the European Convention on Human Rights
- International Criminal Court: www.icc-cpi.int–The ICC investigates and, where warranted, tries individuals charged with the gravest crimes of concern to the international community: genocide, war crimes and crimes against humanity

Now test yourself

TESTED

1 Name the Convention that the HRA incorporated into UK law in 1998.
2 Name the organisation that oversees the operation of the Geneva Conventions.
3 Identify two reasons why the UNDHR is important.
4 Identify an aim of International Humanitarian Law.

Answers online

Exam practice

Human rights abuse

Since 2011, the civil war in Syria has led to many people being forced out of their homes and having to live abroad. Both sides have killed many non-combatants and the Syrian government has been accused of using chemical weapons on its fellow citizens.

1 Consider the ways in which international humanitarian law seeks to protect the non-combatants described in the source. [4]
2 The United Nations Declaration of Human Rights was agreed in 1948, nearly 70 years ago. Present a case to justify changes you would make to its content to make it fit for the next 70 years. [8]
3* Justify the arguments put forward by those UK politicians who wish the UK to withdraw from the European Convention on Human Rights.
In your answer you should consider:
- the content of the European Convention on Human Rights and how it operates
- the reasons why some UK politicians are unhappy with the way the ECHR operates. [8]

ONLINE